Europe's
Franco-German
Engine

SAIS EUROPEAN STUDIES

Europe's Franco-German Engine

David P. Calleo and
Eric R. Staal, editors

Brookings Institution Press
Washington, D.C.

WASHINGTON FOUNDATION FOR EUROPEAN STUDIES

WFES is an educational foundation devoted to encouraging good relations between the United States and Europe through the mutual study of contemporary issues.

The Foundation has pursued its aims in close collaboration with the European Studies Department at the PAUL H. NITZE SCHOOL OF ADVANCED INTERNATIONAL STUDIES (SAIS) of THE JOHNS HOPKINS UNIVERSITY, including its BOLOGNA CENTER in Italy. Besides developing and funding the SAIS European Studies series, WFES supports the regular SAIS European Lecture Series. It also manages the Michael M. Harrison Fund that subsidizes opera and ballet tickets for SAIS students in Bologna and Washington, and encourages a series of informal seminars in Bologna on the historical significance of the opera.

WFES is incorporated in the District of Columbia, and enjoys a 501(c)(3) tax status. Anyone desiring to contribute to its work, or to be invited to the SAIS European Lecture Series, should contact Nancy Tobin at SAIS European Studies, 1619 Massachusetts Avenue, N.W., Washington, D.C. 20036. Contributions should be made out to WFES and are deductible to the amounts permitted by law.

EARLIER WFES STUDIES:

Italy and the United States: National Interests and Shared Values
The International Spectator 31 (April-June 1996).
Joint project with Center for Strategic and International Studies and Istituto Affari Internazionali. The International Spectator is a regular publication of I.A.I.

The New Germany in the New Europe
SAIS Review 15, Special Issue (Fall 1995).

France in the New European and World Order
SAIS Review 13, Special Issue (Fall 1993).

From the Atlantic to the Urals: National Perspectives on the New Europe
Seven Locks Press: Arlington, VA, 1992.

Recasting Europe's Economies: National Strategies in the 1980s
University Press of America: Lanham, MD, 1990.

Additional copies of all volumes may be ordered from:

WASHINGTON FOUNDATION FOR EUROPEAN STUDIES
1619 Massachusetts Ave., N.W. Suite 619
Washington, D.C. 20036

Recasting Europe's Economies and From the Atlantic to the Urals may also be ordered from their publishers. France in the New European and World Order and The New Germany in the New Europe may also be obtained from SAIS Review, 1619 Massachusetts Ave., N.W., Washington, D.C. 20036.

A major project on The Future of Transatlantic Relations is being developed.

CONTENTS

FOREWORD

Since the late 1980s, the European Studies program at SAIS (The Johns Hopkins Nitze School of Advanced International Studies, together with WFES (Washington Foundation for European Studies), has published six studies on various aspects of contemporary Europe. This volume explores the Franco-German partnership mainly from the perspectives of the French and Germans themselves.

We have eight authors, three from France, three from Germany, and two Americans. The six European authors have all in one fashion or another been closely involved in managing Franco-German relations in recent years. Their essays were presented at lectures and seminars at SAIS during the fall of 1996 and were revised during the winter and spring of 1997. As usual, the seminars of experts and our own lively students contributed greatly to the whole process. The authors themselves joined in with dedication and good humor.

Funding was arranged through WFES. Major support came from the Robert Bosch Foundation and France's Ministère des Affaires Étrangères, with additional help from the European Commission and SAIS.

This volume is the first to be presented by *SAIS European Studies,* a venture undertaken in collaboration with the Brookings Institution Press.

David P. Calleo
Eric R. Staal
November 1997

INTRODUCTION

David P. Calleo

Historically, France and Germany are improbable partners. Yet they have linked themselves in an increasingly structured "special relationship" that has been the "engine" of European integration. Since the end of the Cold War, the European Union's capacity to meet its new challenges depends heavily on whether the partnership remains vital and durable. Its current state should, therefore, be of great interest to Americans as well as Europeans.

On the whole, however, Americans have not taken much notice of the Franco-German partnership. It does not fit well with our familiar beliefs about Europe: the weakness and disunity of the Europeans, their perpetual need for American leadership, our own "special relationship" with the Germans, the self-defeating ingenuity of the French, etc. But the Maastricht agenda, with its prospect of a common European currency to rival the dollar, has begun to compel greater attention from Americans. That attention focuses on two basic questions: How real is the Franco-German partnership? And how will it affect American interests?

The essays in this volume provide considerable raw material for the answers. They are mostly written by members of those French and German elites who manage and sustain the partnership. Nearly all have been intimately involved in its inner workings. Their essays fall into three broad categories: diplomatic, military and economic, with a French and a German author for each category. For the discerning reader, the essays are full of revealing arguments and perceptions

1

about contemporary Europe and America. All I can do here is note some of the main points.

Our diplomatic essayists are Gilles Andréani, director of the Center for Analysis and Planning at the French Ministry of Foreign Affairs, and Klaus-Peter Klaiber, Head of Policy Planning at the German Ministry of Foreign Affairs. Both have had varied and brilliant careers. Both are also second-generation Franco-German partners, the sons of distinguished diplomats, Jacques Andréani and Manfred Klaiber, who themselves had major roles in developing the partnership earlier on.

Our two security experts are François Heisbourg and Michael Stürmer. Heisbourg is currently Senior Vice President for Strategic Development at Matra Defense, the big French arms and high-technology firm. An *Enarque* like Andréani, Heisbourg was once a special assistant to Charles Hernu, Minister of Defense in the Mauroy and Fabius governments of the 1980s. Thereafter, he headed the International Institute for Strategic Studies in London for several years. He is a prolific author—well-known and respected in Germany as well as in Britain and the United States. His German counterpart, Michael Stürmer, is a professor of history—distinguished author of several books on modern political and cultural history, frequent commentator in leading newspapers at home and abroad, and currently director of one of Germany's major research institutes for strategic studies, Stiftung Wissenschaft und Politik at Ebenhausen.

In the economic category, our authors are Jean-Pierre Landau and Ernst Welteke. Landau is a high civil servant who was a gifted and popular teacher at SAIS in Washington, while serving as the French Executive Director of the IMF and World Bank. Ernst Welteke is the only former politician among our group—a Social Democrat who is head of Hesse's Landeszentralbank, and thereby a member of the governing committee of the Bundesbank. To these three French and three German authors, we add Patrick McCarthy, our SAIS colleague at the Johns Hopkins Bologna Center and a noted student of European politics, political economy, and culture. McCarthy's essay amplifies our study of the partnership by situating it in the foreign policy and domestic politics of the two countries and noting how other big European states, Italy in particular, view it.

All the essays were written before the French elections of May and June 1997. Their primary purpose is to describe the essence of the relationship as it has evolved over three decades and several governments, including the persistent inner conflicts between the partners. A new French government can be expected to bring changes, but it is too early to speak of any of them with any assurance. It is not impossible, of course, that France and Germany, if increasingly frustrated, may grow alienated from each other, and abandon their joint European project. If so, it would constitute a major revolution in world affairs. The reasons this could happen should be clear to any discerning reader of these essays—and even more the reasons that work strongly to prevent such a revolution, regardless of who is in power in either country.

Gilles Andréani, our first author, opens by directly addressing the basic American questions—the partnership's reality and its implications for others:

> For either the French or the Germans, the Franco-German relationship is a difficult subject to address in front of a foreign public. The relationship has become so central and so obvious, that it is hardly discussed in depth. By contrast, third countries tend to regard it with appreciation, but also with mixed feelings. They recognize it as a key element to the stability of Europe and the conduct of the European Union's policies. They also, at times, show some impatience at what they perceive as the systematic and exclusive character of the relationship. And, occasionally, they question it in a more fundamental way, wondering whether behind the appearance of friendship and closeness, interests are not going to diverge, once again, between France and Germany.

Andréani admits the complexity and elusiveness of a partnership between two nations with such distinct characteristics and with a history of such violent animosity. Their postwar partnership, he says, grew out of a "shared sense of weakness, the instinct that by joining forces they would repair their national self-esteem together." He cites de Gaulle's metaphor of "exhausted and wavering wrestlers which rest against each other." In the same vein, François Heisbourg sees the foundation of the current partnership in "the extreme trauma of utter defeat both countries underwent in 1940 and 1945, respectively."[1] Each played a major role in the misfortunes of the other; fear that the suicidal struggle might recur has been transformed into a deeply rooted incentive for cooperation. In any threat of crisis, Heisbourg observes the two "hold each other more tightly, since a close embrace makes a parting of ways more difficult." But these feelings, rooted in the wartime trauma, are "vulnerable to the passage of time." Hence, as Andréani argues, the importance of a common project to

> give a relationship steadiness and purpose, allowing it to overcome the emotional ups and downs that are unavoidable no matter how deep the mutual feelings.

That common project has been Europe. Andréani dwells on how de Gaulle wooed the Germans and their European-minded Chancellor, Konrad Adenauer. He analyzes the fourfold rationale that de Gaulle presented for the partnership: The Soviet threat compelled unwavering solidarity between France and Germany. The Atlantic Alliance required a European center of power and prosperity comparable to the U.S. Eventually achieving a stable and united Europe "from the Atlantic to the Urals" required not only the collapse of communist ideology but a strong European Community built around a joint Franco-German policy. Finally, European values needed to be reasserted in the world at large.

France and Germany have continued to have differences over the ultimate nature of Europe's Union and its relationship with the U.S. The differences may be profound, Andréani notes, but their practical significance should not be overestimated. France opposes turning the European Union into "some sort of full-fledged statehood entity," but in reality Germans are no more willing to do this than the French. The French do remain more preoccupied with achieving a "balanced relationship" with the U.S., while the Germans, who visualize "two concentric and complementary circles of solidarity," are less sensitive to transatlantic balance, or perhaps more realistic about ever achieving it. But Andréani sees a growing common realization that transatlantic relations are threatened much more "by Europe's weakness and inability to act than by an excess of self-assertiveness. . . ."

Since the end of the Cold War, the partnership has had to cope with a reunited Germany and a new Russia. Andréani sketches the common strategy that has gradually evolved. The response to a bigger, more eastward-oriented Germany has been to press for a more integrated European Union, sufficiently cohesive and efficient to absorb aspiring members from the old Soviet sphere, but not Russia itself, whose Eurasian character precludes its being integrated into NATO or the EU. Out of these joint perspectives, Andréani sees a common Franco-German vision and an ambitious common program:

> In sum, a West European integration progressively deepened should serve as the essential anchor of stability for the continent as a whole. This process should lead to an ever growing European Union, accepting transfers of sovereignty but continuing to build on the existing nation states and falling short of turning into a new statehood entity. The Union should be opened up to new members under conditions which preserve its strength and cohesiveness. This Union must be seen as consistent with, and reinforcing of the transatlantic alliance. Europe should be whole and free. Russia should take part, recognizing her dual nature as a European and global power.

Europe is, of course, far from realizing such a vision, as Andréani admits. The need to enlarge the EU requires not merely institutional streamlining but a core—"some inner, politically cohesive, center of influence." The two partners have grown much closer to working out the character of that core, including the European Monetary Union. The most serious difficulty, Andréani believes, lies not so much between the European partners, but within each of them, as national publics tend to blame the European Union for the economic failings of their own governments.

As for security matters, both partners recognize that Europe, pursuing its own broader integration, needs to promote a stable environment to its east and south. The different regional priorities of French and Germans (French to the South and Germans to the East) are complementary rather than contradictory, Andréani argues. Similarly, both want a good working relationship with the U.S. and both believe this requires a strong and predictable Europe—only possible if Europe is itself cohesive. American attempts to encourage Germans to assume a "partnership in leadership" with the U.S.

> misjudged Germany's aspirations and how deeply Germany and her European partners, starting with France, are committed to channeling their influence and protecting their interests through European cooperation. . . .

Both countries, Andréani concludes, have largely outgrown their wartime wounds. France is much more a mainstream power and Germany less inhibited in promoting her own national ideas and interests. But both developments strengthen the partnership, which can be sound only to the extent that it reflects "each having fully recovered a healthy national identity."

Klaus-Peter Klaiber professes a similar message. The partnership's numerous bilateral institutions are merely the "tip of the iceberg of a close network of consultation and coordination." French and German diplomats even serve in each other's ministries. "Preservation of this privileged partnership is, for both our countries, *'raison d'État'*." European integration is their joint project. Hardly any initiative for it has not come from the two. Others are sometimes uneasy but recognize that "if France and Germany have found a common denominator it is easier to find a solution which is agreeable to all." The partnership is, as Pompidou once said, *"exemplaire"* not *"exclusif."*

Klaiber sketches the partners' present agenda. Both accept the need to "roll the Western European carpet of stability further East and South." France is more preoccupied with the South and Germany with the East; both realize that Europe requires stability in both directions. Enlargement is also vital to restoring Europe's flagging competitiveness. But enlargement also means strengthening the inner coherence of the Union. France and Germany have submitted joint proposals—including the creation of a European planning and analysis center for foreign policy and the appointment of a single person, responsible to the Union's Council of Ministers, to speak and act on behalf of that foreign policy. Europe must also develop a "European military capacity," Klaiber argues, by linking the Western European Union and the EU, a capacity that means Europe could "field a force of its own," should it happen that "the U.S. decides its interests are not involved and prefers not to engage its own forces." This does not mean a turning away from NATO. On the contrary, it "is through NATO and by using NATO resources that we want to organize our European capabilities in the security field." France's move toward reintegration into NATO greatly facilitates the process.

France and Germany are firmly behind the idea of a "flexibility clause" among EU states that would permit some members to proceed more quickly in one or another dimension of European integration. With more and more members and diverging interests, such a capacity is needed to push ahead with integration. The aim is "to give new dynamism to integration, not create a core Europe." "The EU's uniform institutional framework must remain intact" and "no member state wishing to participate should be excluded." Klaiber sees European Monetary Union as "perhaps the most important Franco-German initiative for Europe," and essential to exploit the advantages of a single market. As the biggest exporters within that market, France and Germany have a natural interest in ending currency fluctuations that "cause enormous economic losses." Germany has a special interest: the German mark, the world's second reserve currency, is "overburdened." Of course, the new euro must itself be stable, which has induced both countries to swallow "the bitter pill of reducing their budget deficits." Klaiber agrees with the French Foreign Minister in the Juppé government, Hervé de Charette: EMU is above all a political project to "make European integration irreversible."

The relative skeptic among our three German writers is the historian Michael Stürmer, who writes about security cooperation. The two nations have fundamentally different political characters,

Stürmer argues. Nationhood has been the French form of political existence since Louis XIV and the Revolution, whereas the Germans, despite reunification, "fear the nation state," with which their experiences have been unedifying, and "hope for redemption through European integration." If the demands of the modern world permitted, Stürmer suggests, Germans would consider themselves merely "a collection of tribes with a common vernacular. They have found their true postwar vocation in the 'welfare state'—with their egregious "environmental virtue, and a 'culture of restraint'." Under such circumstances, postwar Franco-German security cooperation can best be described after an old French song: *Two Dreams in One Bed.*

The partnership, Stürmer admits, has nevertheless functioned well, "oiled through an abundance of ministerial meetings, summits, and symbolism, not to mention some eminently practical friendships." The two countries have found the European Union "a convenient framework both to enhance and to disguise their national interest." Nevertheless, Franco-German differences of identity and interest are clearly reflected in the security sphere. After World War II, France was torn between policies of containing Germany and containing the Soviet Union. The U.S. protectorate resolved the problem. But NATO was no help to France beyond Europe, and it was left to de Gaulle to renounce the "bloody stardust of empire" and heal the wounded national ego. To do so, he had to lead France back to the table of the great powers, an aim he pursued through building a strictly national nuclear deterrent, as opposed to the collective European deterrent favored by his predecessors.

Germany, meanwhile, found its national interest in multilateralism. Whereas Germans saw their old nation state "as a nightmare to be put into the archives of history," "Atlanticism and Europe became the beacons of a better future. . . ." They learned that they could "gain more leverage through international institutions, above all NATO and the European Union, than through any isolated national role." Under the circumstances, French military strategy, emphasizing strictly national deterrence and refusing subordination in NATO, "put heavy strains on the Franco-German security relationship. . . ." While the

1980s saw improvements in Franco-German security cooperation, the basic differences remained. They continued to be resolved by American hegemony—containing both the Soviet Union and Germany, while nevertheless providing the Germans with a strategic voice through NATO.

After the "Two plus Four" negotiations had unified Germany and "closed the books on World War II," NATO and the Cold War no longer provided an organizing framework for Franco-German security relations. A new definition was required and the European Union, "an economic framework in search of political purpose," became the arena for finding it. The EU had "to grow into a foreign policy role, or remain forever a free trade zone de luxe." The agenda France and Germany developed together was EMU, the prime French objective, and Political Union, the German aim. EMU got a better start, since it inherited the EU's several decades of economic accomplishment. By contrast, Political Union—including a common foreign and security policy—has inherited the old ambivalence. "Philosophically and politically the two countries, although living within the same strategic space, see themselves in different worlds and react through different and not necessarily complementary strategies." The Germans believe in "architecture" and want to build "a secure neighborhood" by extending NATO and the EU. The French, more pessimistic still, believe in military deterrence and, if necessary, intervention. Both see the need to cooperate, particularly in preserving their arms industries. But the Germans remain "reluctant sellers of arms . . . while the French prefer a more robust approach."

"Both countries, as in the past, build their security on NATO." Europe continues its game of "everybody for himself and the United States for us all." The EU will thus remain for some time an economic giant and a political dwarf, Stürmer believes. The situation should not be without its attractions for Washington, which can use it to "secure a controlling stake in Europe at a modest price." In any event, so long as the U.S. protects the Europeans from "the consequences of their disunity, no existential need will arise, nor the vital energy to forge a power on the European side of the Atlantic." Stürmer nevertheless concludes: "But the rendezvous with reality cannot wait forever." To see the Franco-German partnership as "the organizing principle of a major player on the world scene, called Europe, requires an act of faith."

Stürmer's French partner, François Heisbourg, takes the same history but cautiously arrives at more optimistic conclusions. Unlike Stürmer, he stresses the commonality of historical experience—the parallels in each country's humiliation, near annihilation and unexpected redemption. Fear of a return to the old antagonism, Heisbourg believes, has helped cement the postwar relationship. Moreover, both countries, increasingly interdependent economically, have had to cooperate to shape Western Europe's economic and political order in a fashion conducive to their interests. A "grand bargain" has resulted in the European Community's political and economic sphere, despite the persisting differences between Adenauer's federalist vision and de Gaulle's *Europe des patries.*

Military cooperation has been relatively slow to develop. Aside from some important military-industrial cooperation, serious defense collaboration did not begin until the 1980s. But in 1982, Heisbourg notes, the conjuncture of Mitterrand with Kohl and Genscher, with Hernu and Wörner as Defense Ministers, favored a new climate. Kohl began declaring that Germany's choice was not between Paris and Washington, but for both. Mitterrand endorsed NATO's "double track" strategy and dramatically supported Kohl before the *Bundestag* in January 1983 on the deployment of American missiles in response to the Soviet SS-20s. "A burgeoning of initiatives" led to joint military units and maneuvers, while French nuclear defense doctrines were altered to allay German sensitivities.

German reunification and the Soviet collapse opened a more troubled period, but one that resulted in the Maastricht Treaty, a major upgrading of joint aspirations for closer European integration. Germany saw in Maastricht a way to avoid "re-nationalization" of its foreign and security policy. An upgraded West European Union could be both "the military arm of Europe" and the "European pillar of NATO." Hence, Germany would not have to choose between Paris and Washington. Meanwhile, a Eurocorps with 50,000 soldiers was announced in Bonn in October 1992. France, Heisbourg admits, saw itself the loser in the bilateral balance after the Cold War had ended. Not only was Germany now considerably larger, which the French quickly realized was a mixed blessing for German strength, but France's own greatest asset in the bilateral balance—its independent nuclear deterrent—was devalued. By contrast, Germany's greatest asset—the strong mark—seemed more important than ever. France set out acquiring the same stability for itself, hence, France's devotion to EMU.

Heisbourg goes on to describe how French and German military policies have been converging rapidly in the 1990s. Germany has gradually eliminated obstacles to its forces' participating in allied operations. France has rejoined NATO's Military Committee—to participate in the "renovation and Europeanization of the Alliance's integrated structure." The election of President Chirac, however, has brought this coalescing trend into question. France's radical reconfiguring of its military forces—necessary and sensible in substance but done with no consultation—provoked vigorously negative German reactions. France seemed to be focusing on "out of area" emergencies while abandoning European territorial defense. Numerous high-level meetings have contained some of the damage, Heisbourg believes, and the trend toward convergence of defense perspectives should resume: "France, Germany and the U.K. have been working hand-in-glove on the reform of NATO," and all three have "responded vigorously and successfully against U.S. attempts . . . to water down a previously negotiated agreement on Combined Joint Task Forces."

Heisbourg admits, however, that it is the broader political, economic and diplomatic agenda of building a European Union that carries military cooperation forward. He sees three linked developments likely to determine whether European integration will persist: the success or failure of EMU, the success or failure of enlarging NATO and the EU, and the consequences of generational changes in the two countries.

A successful EMU should have indirect but major consequences for security and defense, Heisbourg believes. With EMU, both France and Germany will embrace a broad vision "of further European integration ... that will rebound on politico-military affairs." "The real question is whether the political and social traffic, notably in France, will bear the increasingly tough disciplines implied by the move to a single currency."

The enlargement of NATO and the EU pose comparable challenges. Heisbourg, not initially in favor of early NATO enlargement, now feels it is inevitable. As he sees it, two sets of issues result for Franco-German cooperation, in the EU as well as in NATO. "The Franco-German couple will have to engage in coalition-building to insure the primacy of its initiatives." Transforming the partnership into "a threesome with the U.K." would make military sense but would require that the U.K. have a similar approach toward security integration, which is not now the case, Heisbourg admits.

Some experts fear that enlargement will polarize French and German strategic concerns but the dangers are easily overstated, Heisbourg argues. The more significant issue is whether Europe should have a "low-profile external intervention policy," or follow the high-profile, "interventionist practice of the U.S., France and the U.K. from 1990 to 1995." Heisbourg sees French and German views converging. The French are growing more wary of interventions. To save money and have more effective forces, the French military is scaling down its external posture. Meanwhile, Germans have been growing more willing and able to participate in coalition operations. "The real divergences may place reluctant Europeans at odds with cantankerous Americans." The French and German partners agree both on the need for NATO reform and on the desirability of an active U.S. presence in European security affairs. Both also share doubts about whether American governments after the Cold War will have sufficient attention or authority to provide Europe with a reliable partner, let alone a hegemon.

Today's collaboration between France and Germany must be assessed, Heisbourg believes, against "the backdrop of changing generations." The relationship has been turned into an operating partnership by a series of extraordinary leaders who have got on well together.

How European and Franco-German will Chancellor Kohl's successor be? How will moving the capital from Bonn to Berlin affect the perspectives of German policy-makers? Like the Anglo-American special relationship, the Franco-German partnership was forged from a trauma whose memory is fading. Thus, even more than in the past, Franco-German collaboration is likely to draw its vitality and overcome its differences only so long as there remains the common European project.

That common European project now depends heavily, all our authors agree, on the fate of Europe's Monetary Union, the most ambitious joint Franco-German undertaking since the founding of the EEC itself. Not surprisingly, the prospects for EMU are the principal preoccupation of our two economic authors, Jean-Pierre Landau and Ernst Welteke. Landau sees two ways of looking at EMU, one optimistic and one pessimistic. Landau firmly joins the optimists. In addition to its many political advantages, EMU has a strong economic rationale, upon which Landau agrees that it ought to be judged. As the critics point out, Landau notes, Europe is not an "optimum currency area." Cultural differences are a powerful impediment to labor mobility, while wages are not diverse and flexible enough to compensate. But the economic case for EMU rests on other considerations, he argues. Without the single currency, it will not be possible to achieve the full benefits expected from the Single Market. Europe's economies are now more highly integrated than some regions of the U.S., but the expected gains from more rational resource allocation can easily be wiped out when relative prices among Europe's states are subject to unpredictable internal currency movements. And, as the disarray of Europe's currencies indicated in September 1992 and July 1993, it is impossible to combine free capital movements with a stable system of narrow bands among separate EU currencies, even when national monetary policies and inflation rates are convergent. The choice for Europe is therefore between EMU and "potential exchange rate instability"—in other words, between a promising future and an unstable status quo.

Landau sketches that promising future. As the risk from volatile internal exchange rates disappears, Europe should benefit from lower interest rates and significant capital inflows. EMU would create a very large financial market in European instruments—of a size, liquidity and depth that would eventually equal the dollar market; financial institutions operating in euros would enjoy numerous competitive opportunities. The dynamics of a unified financial market would strongly favor further economic integration.

To achieve EMU, Landau admits, requires strong political will in both France and Germany. Inflation rates and economic cycles have largely converged, and fiscal policy is also converging, but high unemployment plagues both countries. Certain French academic and political elites blame this unemployment on the *franc fort* and some American academics encourage their reasoning. But joblessness in France, Landau asserts, does not result from the strong currency but mainly from rigid labor markets. Delaying EMU can only make the situation worse by letting speculation add a premium to interest rates.

Landau implies that there are some troubling weaknesses in the Maastricht Treaty's provisions. There is an anomalous division of authority—with the European Central Bank responsible for monetary policy and the Council of Ministers for exchange-rate policy. If the euro's exchange rate is strong, as expected, and some EU members who remain outside EMU allow their currencies to depreciate against it, the less competitive EMU members may be hurt. He expects, however, that there will be strong pressures on all EU members to adhere. A similar problem may arise, he notes, if the euro is strong against non-European currencies, like the dollar. More flexible national labor markets would help make EMU members competitive, Landau argues, even against rivals with depreciated currencies; so would more disciplined fiscal policies. Fiscal policy might, however, be usefully employed to compensate partially for shocks with asymmetric effects within the EU. He agrees there are very good reasons for insisting on the same fiscal limits for every country, but suggests that using a structural rather than current fiscal balance might have been considered so as to adjust for business-cycle fluctuations. He believes the stability pact adopted in 1996 will remedy some of these problems and hopes that it will improve the quality of the EMU's economic policy decision making. Governments should keep open, he adds, the possibilities for absorbing asymmetric shocks through coordinated moves in national budgets. In the U.S., he notes, roughly 35 percent of any shock occuring in a single state is compensated automatically through the federal budget. Without a comparable federal budget, EMU will need effective coordination among national budgets. Landau closes by a plea for close cooperation between French and German governments in stressing to their electorates the urgent need for structural reform and "the commonality of challenges and purposes that our two countries share."

Landau's German colleague, Ernst Welteke, shares his enthusiasm for EMU and is particularly concerned with how it will improve the competitive position of its members against the challenges of globalization and the repeated shocks of abrupt changes in the external value of the dollar and changes "whose causes may or may not be economically based." For Germany and France, dollar shocks are greatly magnified by their uneven effects on the various European currencies. A falling dollar invariably means a greater appreciation of the mark than of the lira or the pound. German trade with Italy and Britain is much larger than with the U.S. and German domestic prices are correspondingly disturbed. An EMU of fifteen members would greatly reduce Germany's vulnerability. The EU's exports currently equal 28 percent of GDP and its imports 26 percent. "In a united Europe of 15 states these figures would fall to eleven percent." In other words, a solid European currency bloc would give its members much better protection against the vagabond dollar.

EMU, Welteke predicts, will also cut transaction costs, make prices transparent and calculations for long-term investment easier. It will attract capital and make it easier for smaller firms to find investment funds. A certain "competition of systems" will follow among European states. Rigid structures will be easier to crack open. A fiscal stability pact will complement the monetary union and favor fiscal retrenchment—now needed with or without EMU. In addition, EMU will discipline the EU's enlargement. Aspiring members will have to prepare their economies—a process that will require important economic changes even for relatively advanced states like the Czech Republic and Hungary. The best might qualify in ten years, Welteke observes.

Our essays certainly make clear how much is riding on EMU. The whole European project seems hostage to its success. Yet its difficulties are formidable. The accumulated excesses of the European welfare state, together with far-reaching economic changes in the world at large, are undermining Europe's whole postwar political and economic formula of welfare capitalism. Meeting austere criteria for fiscal and inflationary limits is, according to conventional wisdom, the only appropriate prescription for Europe's declining competitiveness. Welfare states need to go on a severe diet. EMU's criteria impose such a regime on fiscal spending. Renouncing devaluation, moreover, means that easing unemployment depends more than ever on achieving more flexible labor markets, i.e., lower wages. Given this conventional wisdom, French and German efforts to impose EMU on Europe's other states, as well as on their own citizens seems an extraordinarily courageous exercise of political will, quite contrary to customary views about the timidity of political leadership in Europe.

Even if EMU is opportune economically, it is problematic politically. With today's very high unemployment and increasingly skewed income distribution, EMU's prescriptions are bound to appear as attacks on the postwar gains of the workforce, and be resisted for that reason. The Maastricht prescriptions, moreover, do not seem to be working to relieve Europe's mounting unemployment. Reactions to unemployment are, therefore, taking an anti-European form.

McCarthy's essay elaborates on the reasons: mounting apprehension among publics over the consequences of further integration for living standards and job security, resurgent nationalism as a protective reaction, disaffection with leaders and elites insensitive to these fears, opportunism among competing politicians eager to take advantage of the situation. As he makes vividly clear, the partners' grand EMU project risks a great fall.

Why have French and German leaders chosen to play for such high stakes? McCarthy weaves together the circumstances, general and adventitious, that led Mitterrand, Kohl, and now Chirac to commit so much political capital to the European monetary enterprise. The outcome presumably depends greatly on how well the two governments, and their neighbors, can meet their own Maastricht criteria, and with what consequences. More fundamentally, it will probably depend on whether the Franco-German relationship is, at heart, conflictual, as McCarthy more than suspects. Certainly the old conflicts remain. But arguably, France's postwar resurgence has made the relationship more balanced than before. And, as Andréani points out, reunification does not necessarily mean a stronger Germany than previously. The real question is whether the mutual consciousness of larger common interests, global as well as European, now overrides these old European quarrels.

Most of our French and German authors strongly imply that this is so. Welteke and Klaiber, as we have seen, add some further geoeconomic reasons to the usual liberal rationale. Welteke dwells on the combined weight of the closely integrated French and German national economies. Together they account for 15 percent of the world's production, 17 percent of its trade, and 14 percent of all its foreign direct investment. Welteke also dwells on the huge size of the European Single Market and the opportunities that a corresponding capital market will create for Europe's financial firms. Like Welteke, Klaiber also notes how fluctuations of exchange rates "cause enormous economic losses," and how Germany is particularly "overburdened" because of the mark's role as a world reserve currency and, therefore, has an "additional interest in creating the euro."

In plainer terms, the German economy is suffering increasingly from an overvalued national currency, caused in good part by frequent manipulations of the dollar. Thoughtful Germans realize they should get rid of today's mark, provided they can do so without entering into inflationary adventures with their more frivolous neighbors. After their reflationary fling in the early 1980s, the French have been anything but frivolous about inflation. Their elites have convinced themselves that their country's economic health requires a strong currency. Hence the partners' grand project of EMU.

McCarthy's essay, which closes our volume, gives a good feel for the complex dynamics in the relationship—between the differing diplomatic and economic perspectives and interests, and the domestic politics of each country. He discusses the bad as well as good phases of the relationship which he sees, in any case, as essentially conflictual. He seems more pessimistic than most of our French and German authors who, at our meetings, seemed to share an impressive congruence of basic views and a relaxed approach to their differences. They all spoke of a profound determination not to let the relationship fail—for reasons of mutual self-interest. This is understood perhaps best of all among politicians and especially among the top civil servants in both countries. Nevertheless, as McCarthy makes clear, and the other essays do not minimize, the difficulties that the partnership must address are formidable, in a world that seems to offer challenges to Europe from all sides.

But while the difficulties are formidable, it would be unfair not to recognize how much the partnership has accomplished, and it would be unwise, I expect, to underestimate its potential for the future. As Welteke notes, a European monetary bloc would create a large, integrated and relatively autarkic continental economy, whose market would be no more exposed to fluctuations of foreign currencies than the American market itself. With EMU, Europeans could be more like the Americans, in other words relatively indifferent to a declining exchange rate. Some reasons are left unspoken. Perhaps the Germans, with their rapidly growing debt and high unemployment, would someday like to try a little reflation—American style. EMU would certainly provide more options for economic policy. It should also provide more power to shape the world's financial system. As Klaiber does note clearly enough: "The European currency will over time change international capital markets. The U.S. dollar will feel the effects. My advice to America is: familiarize yourselves with the idea of a strong and stable European currency." Klaiber concludes by again quoting the former French Foreign Minister Hervé de Charette: "*La monnaie, c'est bien entendu un projet politique.*" Klaiber adds: The common currency "will lead us one big step further towards the great Franco-German vision of the economic and political Union of Europe, a Europe which will be a strong partner for America."

What should Americans make of this? Instead of a divided and weak dependency, is Europe to become a strong and cohesive rival? Is this the vision behind France and Germany's European project? Is such a Europe what we really want? Should we, as Dr. Klaiber argues, welcome "a strong partner for America?" Or should we, as Professor Stürmer suggests, draw comfort from Europe's disunity? For a long time, our skepticism about Europe's capacity has shielded us from having to decide.

The answer depends, among other things, on what vision we Americans have of ourselves in the future. Are we to be the Romans of the Third Millennium, or should we aspire to a more modest role? This is a question that history has been asking Americans, on and off, throughout much of the twentieth century. The Cold War era allowed us to avoid answering it clearly. As in both the world wars, we were presumably preventing the hegemony of another rather than establishing our own. But in the process of containing the Soviets, we also helped to build up Europe and Japan, allies against Soviet influence but also rivals in the new global economy that we were fostering. The end of the Cold War both sharpens and obscures the issue.

The American can think of his country as the only "superpower" in a "unipolar" world, and wonder why that world needs a cohesive and strong Europe. At present we are still enjoying our peace dividend from the collapse of Soviet power. Our traditional NATO military burdens have suddenly grown much cheaper. For the first time since the 1970s, it is possible to imagine a balanced federal budget in the near future. But in a larger and longer geopolitical view, one that encompasses American responsibilities in Asia as well as Europe during the coming century, a strong Europe, able to look after itself and pull its weight in the world, has its attractions. Those who like such a prospect should rejoice at the strength of the Franco-German partnership, and be solicitous of its future.

THE FRANCO-GERMAN RELATIONSHIP IN A NEW EUROPE

Gilles Andréani

For either the French or the Germans, the Franco-German relationship is a difficult subject to address in front of a foreign public. The relationship has become so central and so obvious, that it is hardly discussed in depth. By contrast, third countries tend to regard it with appreciation, but also with mixed feelings. They recognize it as a key element to the stability of Europe and the conduct of the European Union's policies. They also, at times, show some impatience at what they perceive as the systematic and exclusive character of the relationship. And, occasionally, they question it in a more fundamental way, wondering whether behind the appearance of friendship and closeness, interests are not going to diverge, once again, between France and Germany.

Skepticism is, I believe, more apparent in the United States than anywhere else. There is a certain American pessimism about Europe, according to which the essential instinct of the Europeans has always been power. Were it not for the American presence and influence, the Europeans would inevitably revert to the poisons of power politics; traditional alliances and rivalries would form again as they allegedly did in the former Yugoslavia. This view, once referred to by a senior German diplomat as "the Spenglerian-Kissinger school of thought," is fundamentally flawed: it ignores the accomplishments of the Franco-German relationship, underestimates the dynamics of the European integration process, and, incidently, is a misperception of what really happened in the former Yugoslavia.

I won't try to dispel that pessimistic view directly. As much as I believe in the soundness and quality of our bilateral relationship with Germany, I would rather draw your attention to the underlying ambitions which we share with Germany and Europe. Feelings and friendship matter in international relations, but, as with a couple, shared interests and a common project give a relationship steadiness and purpose, allowing it to overcome the emotional ups and downs that are unavoidable no matter how deep the mutual feelings.

De Gaulle's Vision

Among nations, as well as among people, there are defining moments. For the Franco-German relationship no period mattered more than the late 1950s and early 1960s; that is, from Adenauer's first visit to de Gaulle in September 1958 to the signature of the Franco-German Treaty in January 1963. In between, the French president and German Chancellor met fourteen times and established a deep personal relationship. Not only did they manage to convey to their respective nations the sense of mutual respect and trust which they had developed between them, but they developed a vision of what the Franco-German relationship was about, that is to say, Europe.

Nothing was less natural than the de Gaulle-Adenauer relationship. Adenauer had previously developed a natural understanding with another French statesman, Robert Schuman, who shared his Christian Democratic convictions and his vision of a Federal Europe, two features, needless to say, totally alien to de Gaulle's vision of Europe. This, I believe, should give us a clue to the essence of the Franco-German relationship: it is not a natural meeting of minds, but a shared will to overcome differences that at times may be significant.

For de Gaulle, this will was never as apparent and successful as during his visit to Germany in September 1962, which was the culminating point of this defining period. It is worth remembering the atmosphere of the visit, and how de Gaulle staged it. An old man of 73 years, he took it upon himself to memorize six speeches in German, a language which he mastered with difficulty. All those speeches are filled with respect and admiration for Germany, for the German worker when addressing the Thyssen factories, and for the German soldier in front of the German War College. *Der Spiegel,* then as now not a characteristically francophile newspaper, commented: "De Gaulle arrived as President of France and left as Emperor of Europe."

De Gaulle was the quintessential politician. Nothing was further from him than indulging in a spontaneous display of feelings. The emotions he stirred were meant to serve a strategic vision, which he exposed on September 4, 1962, in a speech worth reading again because it contains essentially everything which the Franco-German relationship has since accomplished.

I won't try to translate de Gaulle's flamboyant rhetoric, but rather stress his main points. After evoking the reconciliation between the two countries, which he compares to "exhausted and wavering wrestlers which rest against each other," he goes on to give four reasons why they should go beyond reconciliation to form a union. First, the common Soviet threat calls for unwavering solidarity between France and Germany. Second, the strength of the Atlantic alliance depends on a European center of power and prosperity comparable to the United States. Third, a Europe "from the Atlantic to the Urals," has two preconditions: in the East, an end to "the dominating ambitions of an obsolete ideology;" and in the West, "a European Community strong and alive, that is to say, essentially, a single and joint Franco-German policy." Fourth, the world needs European values, in particular the values of Germany and France.

De Gaulle was to leave this agenda unfulfilled to a large extent. At the time, members of the European Community did not manage to overcome their differences on three issues, which, incidentally, are not totally irrelevant to today's European debate: the nature of the political union which de Gaulle contemplated for Western Europe, whether Great Britain should be allowed into it, and the relationship of the new entity with the United States. The Franco-German rapprochement culminated in January 1963 in the signing at the Elysée of a bilateral treaty of cooperation. But this achievement was clouded by the outcome of the ratification process in Germany, which ended with the Bundestag's deliberately contradicting de Gaulle's approach to those three issues. Even so, the Franco-German agenda laid out by de Gaulle in 1962 remains relevant. It was pursued through the accomplishments and vicissitudes of successive French governments and can still be used today as a thread to guide us through past results and for our future ambitions.

Reconciliation

Before going on to de Gaulle's four aims, let me first address the issue of reconciliation itself. There was nothing exceptional in calling for reconciliation in postwar Europe. Churchill had, in his Zürich Speech in 1946, called for "a blessed act of oblivion" and stressed that "the first step in the recreation of a European family must be a partnership between France and Germany." Indeed, well before de Gaulle, the seeds of reconciliation had been planted by private groups and church leaders, promoting youth exchanges and cultural dialogue. The results were reflected in the 1963 Franco-German Treaty which established machinery for such exchanges and still functions to this day.

The quality of the results is impressive, even in the pacified environment of today's Europe. Polls show that more than seventy percent of the French public regard Germany as their closest ally, a status unsurpassed by any other country. Similar figures are achieved among the German public, where France comes second only to the United States.

These polls suggest that there was something deeper about the French-German reconciliation than about any comparable process among other European countries. De Gaulle's image of exhausted wrestlers gives us one possible explanation: the two countries shared a common weakness. Germany had been physically and morally destroyed by the war. France was, technically speaking, among the victors, but victory was not hers. Throughout her history France not only felt the mistress of her own fate, but also indulged in the dream that through her ideas, culture and, occasionally, sheer force, she could shape Europe and the world to her image. But de Gaulle in 1962, far from being the Emperor described by *Der Spiegel*, was the leader of a country that had lost its dreams and been brought to the brink of civil war by two years of colonial conflict. His main task was to restore to France a sense of self-confidence.

I find it a telling human story, as well as a matter of wonder in the conduct of international relations, that at the roots of the Franco-German relationship should lie this shared sense of weakness, the instinct that by joining forces they would repair their national self-esteem together. That instinct does much to explain the enduring and exceptional strength of the relationship.

To be sure, France and Germany chose, if not different roads, at least different styles in order to assert their place in the world against this unfavorable background. While the strategic choices were essentially the same, i.e. belonging to the Western alliance and further-ing European integration, the methods formed quite a contrast. The Federal Republic never was a political dwarf. Since its creation it possessed significant weight and influence to further national interests that were very clearly defined. But Adenauer's Germany always had a preference for pursuing objectives through collective action and multilateral force, and felt an instinctive revulsion to acting alone, or at least to being isolated. France, under General de Gaulle and his successors, never hesitated to stress what made her different. A claim for national independence made France distance herself in 1966 from the NATO military structure, and generally made her impatient with the leadership role of the United States. France's conviction that she embodies universal aspirations made her pursue original policies towards the Third World in the 1970s and 1980s.

That such diverging styles should, at times, cause misperceptions and frictions between France and Germany was unavoidable. The Germans, who praised predictability and reliability above all, were, more than once, surprised by French initiatives. The French, for their part, feared that the Germans' compulsion never to be at odds with their main international partners led them to undertake conflicting commitments, or at least to reconcile such commitments in a fashion that eroded their capacity for intellectual clarity. But the Franco-

German relationship was never meant to turn the French into Germans or vice-versa, and the strength of the relationship does not depend on doing so. The difference in national characters hopefully remains. The important thing is that those differences were always acknowledged and respected on both sides, and were never pushed so far as to jeopardize the reconciliation process itself.

Solidarity in the Cold War

First on General de Gaulle's agenda was France and Germany's solidarity in the face of the Soviet threat. Our common accomplishments in this respect now belong to history, and I won't dwell on them. They include de Gaulle's unflinching solidarity with Adenauer at the time of the Berlin crisis, President Giscard d'Estaing's close understanding with Chancellor Schmidt on the "dual track" approach to the Euromissile issue and, on the same subject, President Mitterrand's address to the Bundestag in 1983, when, in the face of the SPD's opposition, he gave decisive support to the deployment of American nuclear missiles in Germany.

An important offshoot from the latter episode was the decision of the two governments to implement the military clauses of the 1963 treaty. As a result, a joint defense council was established in 1988 and a new impulse was given to practical military cooperation. At the same time it was decided to create a Franco-German brigade, a project later expanded into the Eurocorps. In parallel with such bilateral initiatives, the two countries decided in 1984 to revitalize the Western European Union, which they later agreed to develop as the defense arm of the European Union.

European Integration and Transatlantic Relations

The second of de Gaulle's Franco-German objectives was a West-European center of power and prosperity, within and strengthening the Atlantic alliance. There is no need to stress the role that Germany and France have played in the development of the European Community, including the crucial step of enshrining it in a European Union of much wider ambition, the result of the Maastricht Treaty.

At every stage of West European integration, Franco-German joint action has played a key role. From the precursor of the Community, the High Authority for Coal and Steel (explicitly devised as a tool to further the cooperation between France and Germany), to the creation of European Political Cooperation and the European Monetary System in the 1970s, to the launching of the Single European Market in 1986, to the joint proposal of two Conferences on Monetary and Political Union in 1990, the achievements of Franco-German cooperation are impossible to distinguish from the general progress of European integration.

Have Germany and France all along seen eye to eye as they acted as the driving force in European integration? I believe so in respect to the wider strategic objectives of the process, at least as these objectives were defined in the mid-1950s by the founding fathers of Europe: Jean Monnet, Robert Schuman and Konrad Adenauer. They hoped to create a web of cooperation so intense as to generate "de facto solidarities," not only to make new conflicts unthinkable, but to bring about an "ever closer union" among the peoples of Europe.

France and Germany have shared the sense that European integration was not in conflict with Atlantic solidarity. It is noteworthy that in 1962 de Gaulle saw the two objectives as mutually reinforcing, going so far as to say that West European unity was the condition of an enduring alliance. Beyond this wide strategic convergence, however, two issues have remained unsettled between France and Germany. The first is the nature of the Union which is eventually going to result from the process of European integration. Whereas Germany expresses little doubt that a federal Europe should eventually evolve, France has always been reluctant to endorse the concept. Even the most convinced advocates of European union on the French side shy away from using clearly the language of a truly federal Europe. Jacques Delors refers to a "federation of states," President Giscard d'Estaing to a "federative Europe," and in the Maastricht negotiation, the French government never went further than to refer somehow vaguely to "the federal finality" of the Europe-to-be.

A second unresolved issue is the relationship between Europe and the United States. Beyond the sincere unqualified proposition that a strong and united Europe is the condition of a healthy alliance, France and Germany certainly have different sentiments towards this key issue. The French side has always conceived of Europe as a power in her own right, able to form her positions autonomously and to achieve a balanced relationship with the United States. I assume that Germany tends to perceive of Europe and of the Atlantic alliance more as two concentric and complementary circles of solidarity, and is less sensitive to, or perhaps more realistic about the balanced character of the relationship.

These differences, significant as they are, should not be overestimated. For a federal country like Germany "federalism" is a positive word, which conveys the idea of a balanced distribution of responsibilities between various levels of government. For a unitary state like France, it inevitably carries the intention to turn, at some point, the European Union into some sort of full-fledged statehood entity, a step which, I believe, Germany is not more prepared to take than we are. As for the relationship between Europe and the United States, there is much less to divide France and Germany than there used to be. That the transatlantic relationship is threatened far more in the long run by Europe's weakness and inability to act than by an excess of self-assertiveness seems to me an obvious assessment, one widely shared not only in France and Germany, but also on the American side of the Atlantic.

Europe from the Atlantic to the Urals

Beyond the relatively narrow circle of countries engaged in the West European integration process lies the rest of Europe. As General de Gaulle put it in his prophetic prediction of September 1962, there lies "Europe from the Atlantic to the Urals." His statement was prophetic in two respects. He foresaw that the domination of communism, an "obsolete ideology," would one day fade away from Eastern Europe. He also assumed that the successful reincorporation of these countries into Europe required a strong and united Western Europe, which implied in turn a joint Franco-German policy. This leads to two additional issues: German unification and the place of Russia on our continent.

On German unification let me once more refer to de Gaulle. In his press conference of February 9, 1965, he strongly urged that Germany's fate should no longer be left unsettled and outlined the conditions needed for her unification. Russia would have to renounce totalitarian constraint so that the people in Eastern Europe would be free to play their role in a new Europe. Meanwhile, a settlement among all concerned would have to be achieved on borders and armaments. Finally, there would have to be further progress toward achieving the political cohesion of Western Europe.

Twenty-five years later, the aspirations of the peoples of Eastern Europe for freedom and the decision of the Soviet Union not to use force against them brought about German unity. The French government consistently supported German unification, only insisting that border issues be solved in the context of the settlement. To be sure, we misjudged the pace of events: starting with the fall of the Berlin wall, we thought that a few years would be necessary before unification could be achieved. But this wrong assessment, shared by quite a few in the German government, did not reflect French reluctance or fear, but rather our awareness of the magnitude of the stakes and our conviction that no chances should be taken in bringing the process to a successful conclusion.

The essential contribution of the Franco-German relationship to these momentous events was a joint judgment that German unification should be matched with new progress in European integration. Chancellor Kohl and President Mitterrand called for two intergovernmental conferences on monetary and political union, which were to result in the Maastricht Treaty. They wanted the Western part of Europe to become a pole of attraction for the rest of the continent, and realized that to remain cohesive, it had to be strengthened beforehand. They also felt that the renewed commitment of Germany and France to the European process was the best way to enshrine German unification into the broader vision of a Europe whole and free.

My second issue is Russia. Russia belongs to Europe by virtue of geography, but is, at the same time, much more than a European country. She is both an Asian and global power. The metaphor of a Europe from the Atlantic to the Urals reflects this reality. Russia has a role to play in Europe, but is never going to be tightly integrated into Europe. Immensely important as she is to France, and even more so to Germany, Russia is both inside and outside of Europe. Her role on our continent has to be acknowledged but should be reflected in special arrangements, rather than by opening up to Russia institutions like NATO or the EU, whose geographical and political scope must be confined to strictly European countries.

The Europe whole and free that was realized together with German unification (and of which we had long dreamt) does not come to an end on the border of Russia, much less on the border of Ukraine or Belarus. But proceeding eastward into Russia, Europe does progressively give way to another geographical and human reality, a fact of which, I believe, Germany and France are well aware.

In sum, a West European integration progressively deepened should serve as the essential anchor of stability for the continent as a whole. This process should lead to an ever growing European Union, accepting transfers of sovereignty but continuing to build on the existing nation states and falling short of turning into a new statehood entity. The Union should be opened up to new members under conditions which preserve its strength and cohesiveness. This Union must be seen as consistent with, and reinforcing of the transatlantic alliance. Europe should be whole and free. Russia should take part, recognizing her dual nature as a European and global power. These are the essential features, I believe, of a common Franco-German vision of Europe. As I have tried to demonstrate, this vision was not brought about by accident, or recently. Most of it goes back three or four decades and was developed on both sides with determination, patience and statesmanship. The story is by no means over, and much will have to be done to bring this vision about, all the more because Europe is changing, and facing new risks, which challenge both our vision and our special relationship.

New Challenges

The Franco-German Relationship in an Enlarged Europe

The success of the Franco-German relationship never lay in the fact that the two countries spontaneously agreed on everything. Quite the contrary, it depended on the political will and ability of two essentially different countries to reconcile divergent sensitivities and positions for the sake of a common European vision. France and Germany are themselves countries at Europe's crossroads, at the junction of Southern and Northern Europe, of Protestant and Catholic Europe, of a free-market Europe and a Latin Europe more influenced by statist and mercantilist traditions. Internally, each has had to cope with the dilemmas not very different from those which Europe faces as a whole.

Will France and Germany still be in a position to play this key role in an enlarged Europe, where Germany will inevitably assume a more central role, both by virtue of geography and by the influence and economic weight she naturally carries in Eastern Europe? This was the central strategic problem addressed in a policy paper of Germany's CDU in October 1994, a paper widely held to reflect Chancellor Kohl's own ideas. The answer, according to the paper, is a "core Europe" organized around France, Germany, and the Benelux countries, the same countries which, at the time, seemed most likely to enter phase III of the Economic and Monetary Union in January 1999. The CDU proposal was partly dismissed in France on the grounds that it left aside two key members of the European Union, Spain and Italy, and because the CDU had mentioned the dreadful word "federal" to describe how the "core" should be organized.

However, there is no doubt that enlarging the European Union will require organizing some inner, politically cohesive, center of influence to compensate for the increased membership and diversity. EMU will have a role to play in this respect, although by no means an exclusive one. But this general proposition will have to be implemented very carefully. The core of Europe is not to be determined mainly from debt or inflation ratios. Rather, it should bring together those countries politically most committed to the European integration process. This circle is by no means restricted to the founding members of the EEC (witness Spain) and future members should be allowed to join if they show the same "European spirit."

Such a core should help an enlarged EU preserve its essential features and balance, thereby maintaining the central role of France and Germany. There are two other factors working to preserve the partnership. First, France and Germany are now much closer to defining a joint strategy for enlargement than they were four years ago. Initial German enthusiasm has given way to a more careful approach, while France now fully shares the political assessment that enlargement is vital for Europe's stability and should be pursued with determination. Their will to act jointly in Central and Eastern Europe is evidenced in the vitality of the trilateral cooperation that now engages Poland, Germany and France—the Weimar Triangle. Second, neither partner is resigned to the notion that an enlarged Europe must necessarily be a more diluted one. The two countries agree that the essential objective of the ongoing IGC is to put the institutions of the Union in order before enlargement, and they are working together for that purpose.

Reconciling Public Opinion with European Integration

The vitality of the Franco-German relationship is essentially dependent on the ability of the two countries to promote a European vision which is not only shared by their governments but supported by their publics. In this respect there are many problems which France and Germany have to face. Public opinion ascribes the current economic and fiscal difficulties to the transition to the single currency. There is, besides, a more general feeling that the EU is restricting governments from carrying out the policies for which they have been democratically elected. This feeling engenders a frustration apparent in both countries. It is evidenced in Germany by the insistence on subsidiarity, in particular from the Länder.

Both governments are determined to change these perceptions, to improve the democratic character of the European Union, and to keep a steady course, both on EMU and on the IGC. But it is clear that short of a perceptible improvement in the economic situation, public hostility is going to loom large over the European process.

The Relationship between Europe and the United States

In a global world, European integration cannot be conceived of in isolation. The EU's internal political and economic objectives, i.e., bringing about reconciliation and unity among the peoples of Western Europe and creating a single market, are close to being achieved. More and more, its key objectives are going to be external, e.g., contributing to a stable environment for Europe, both to the South and to the East, and promoting European interests throughout the world.

Nowhere could the European Union contribute more to global stability than in the field of transatlantic relations. Europe will have to deal in the future with an America still committed to Europe, but more uncertain as to the degree, scope, and forms of her commitment. It is vital for Europe to achieve a steady and predictable working relationship with the United States, one that allows both sides of the Atlantic to address jointly the global and regional issues in which they share converging interests.

This is not going to be an easy task. There are, on the one hand, encouraging trends: the new quality of the Franco-American relationship; and the prospect of NATO adapting to a greater and more visible role for the Europeans and Americans to play together. But there are also disturbing factors: the propensity of the United States to resort to unilateral action, and Europe's division and lack of common purpose that emerged in the disintegration of the former Yugoslavia.

In the long run, the key to a stable transatlantic relationship is a cohesive Europe. Thus, when President Bush offered Germany a partnership in leadership or when President Clinton, in August 1994, singled out Germany to assume a leadership role in Europe, I believe they misjudged Germany's aspirations and how deeply Germany and her European partners, starting with France, are committed to channeling their influence and protecting their interests through European cooperation, rather than by any other means.

In addition to furthering Europe's interests, Franco-German cooperation can serve the overall goal of an improved transatlantic relationship: indeed, this will be an essential challenge for both countries as they push the European integration process.

Will the Franco-German Relationship Remain Balanced?

Will the mere size and economic strength of Germany make it difficult, if not impossible, to maintain a sound and healthy relationship with France? Since reunification, this question has been looming over Europe.

Before I tell you what I believe is the key to that question, let me tell you what France will *not* do to address it. She will not try to enlist other countries in a balancing act against Germany. To be sure, there has been a dramatic improvement in our relations with Britain over the last couple of years, in particular in the field of security policy. What prompted us to seek a better relationship is the conviction that Europe needs Britain. We need her global reach and influence, her sense of energy and fighting spirit. Indeed, there will never be a European foreign and security policy worthy of the name if Britain does not participate fully in it. At the same time, we have a European vision, over whose vital elements we cannot compromise. We simply hope to convince Britain that her interests will be best served if channeled through Europe, and that she, therefore, needs to join the Economic and Monetary Union and to commit herself fully to the European Union.

The key to a sound and lasting Franco-German cooperation lies, however, nowhere else but in both countries: in their ability to work steadily, as they have done for more than forty years, to overcome their differences for the sake of Europe. I spoke earlier about their diverging attitudes as both countries tried to repair their national pride in the postwar period. This process is now coming to an end. Both countries have recovered their self-esteem and found a proper place in the world. France is now more of a mainstream power, less prone to affirm herself by dissenting or standing out, and Germany is less inhibited about openly promoting her ideas and interests. Both developments are good news for the Franco-German relationship. On our side, it would be a great mistake to expect to build a balanced and lasting relationship on German guilt and self-abnegation. Quite the opposite, the condition for an enduring relationship lies in each partner's self-confidence and frankness in examining their differences—in a nutshell, in each having fully recovered a healthy national identity.

Like Europe itself, the Franco-German relationship entered a new era with the fall of the Berlin Wall. As the postwar period came to an end, France and Germany had to face a new challenge: how to move beyond their achievements of reconciliation, essentially achieved within a narrow West European community, to a joint vision of an enlarged Europe.

They have engaged to pursue this transition together. Essentially, they have resolved to pursue their old strategy of furthering the European integration process, while adjusting it to the new realities. The main challenge to this strategy does not lie in any underlying disagreement or potential imbalance between France and Germany. It rests with the possible demoralization of their publics confronted with painful economic and fiscal adjustments. Self-confidence and morale will ultimately decide the outcome of this new episode in the Franco-German relationship. The success of that relationship remains critical, not only for both countries, but for Europe as a whole. As Winston Churchill put it in 1946, "there can be no revival of Europe without a spiritually great France and a spiritually great Germany."

EUROPE'S FRANCO-
GERMAN ENGINE: GENERAL
PERSPECTIVES

Klaus-Peter Klaiber

"**A**merica wishes a strong Europe!" This was the message of President Clinton's historic address to the French National assembly in June 1995. The President's message put an end to the old academic dispute of whether or not European integration would alienate us from America. No. European integration and transatlantic partnership were always two sides of the same policy aimed at safeguarding peace, democracy and common values. What the EU achieved during the Cold War—unprecedented political and economic stability in Western Europe—would have been impossible without the backing and the support of the Atlantic Alliance. NATO was and will remain a decisive factor of European stability and security. America must have its place in Europe.

On September 6, 1996, in Stuttgart, Secretary of State Warren Christopher firmly reiterated America's commitment for Europe. He went even further and suggested a "New Atlantic Community." He said: "Closer political cooperation in the European Union, and its coming enlargement, will contribute to the security and prosperity of the New Atlantic Community."[1] Europe is now called upon to live up to its own ambitions and take over its share of responsibility. I know that America is waiting impatiently for a more effective partner called "Europe." Germany and France will work together to achieve this goal. But we should never forget that it has taken the United States of America more than 200 years to become what it is today. United Europe has just covered its first 45 years of growing together.

Talking about Europe is impossible without looking at the Franco-German couple. Exactly 50 years ago, in his famous speech at Zürich University, Churchill called for a united Europe and he had in particular two countries in mind: "The first step in the re-creation of the European family must be a partnership between France and Germany."[2] His suggestion proved to be right. Franco-German reconciliation after the war was the basis for what turned out to be the European Union, the first and still only association of states in the world with shared sovereignty, joint institutions, joint decision-making bodies with majority voting and a joint court of justice. Worldwide, the EU has become a model for peaceful cooperation on a regional scale. It is a unique form of cooperation between nations whose past was abundant with nationalist rivalry and aggression.

No two other countries in the world have developed such close cooperation as Germany and France. Our countries are each other's most important economic partners. On the political level there are at least two summit meetings each year and regular consultations between foreign ministers. Several joint Franco-German institutions, like the Franco-German Council for Defense and Security or the Franco-German Economic and Finance Council, are only the tip of the iceberg of a close network of consultation and coordination. Nearly every day there is a Franco-German meeting on the agenda in Bonn and Paris.

Our embassies exchange reports and carry out joint instructions. French and German diplomats have been integrated into each other's ministries. It is easily possible today at an international conference to find a German speaking from the French chair.

Our friendship is deeply rooted in our peoples. There are more than 1,600 town-twinnings and 3,000 school-partnerships, as well as a youth exchange with more than five million participants. Opinion polls reveal that, for the French, Germany is their country's "best friend" and that, for Germans, France, I hesitate to say, is second only to the United States. The basis for this friendship is the conviction that two big countries like Germany and France, neighbors at the center of Europe but enemies for centuries, must live together peacefully.

The magic formula has been European integration. The underlying principle was revolutionary. Basically, it has not changed: to create interdependence through economic integration, thereby linking each country's own interests with the interests of its neighbors, creating trust, and preventing quarrels. And if there is a quarrel, as recently in the BSE crisis, Europe has a common law and procedures to settle it peacefully. This principle has led to a breakthrough to a new and stable peace order in Western Europe. It has created unprecedented prosperity. For forty years it has been a success story.

Germany and France will continue to be the engine of this process. Our countries have the strongest interest in following such a path. We are, in a way, the hinge that keeps the Union together. General de Gaulle once called our relationship "a marriage of convenience with a considerable amount of feelings." Today, we are like a married couple in their forties. We have lived together through the ups and downs. There are and there will be differences and divergences. But we have learned to put our partnership and our common goal, united Europe, above our national particularities. The preservation of this privileged partnership is, for both our countries, "raison d'état." It is hard to find any initiative for integration in Europe which has not come from our two countries:

- The European Monetary System in 1979
- The Single European Act of 1985, melting together the different lines of integration
- The idea of a single market without tariff barriers
- European Monetary Union which will start at the beginning of 1999
- A Political Union with a Common Foreign and Security Policy
- The Eurocorps based on the Franco-German brigade
- The creation of a European security and defense identity

Our partners in the EU have always welcomed the Franco-German driving force in European integration, even if they sometimes feel a bit uneasy with our numerous joint initiatives. But also for them it is clear that it takes two to tango. If France and Germany have found a common denominator it is easier to find a solution which is agreeable to all. We stick to President Pompidou's solicitous formulation: The Franco-German partnership is meant to be *exemplaire*, not *exclusif*. In the years ahead of us, Europe is facing new challenges which are comparable only to the tasks at the starting phase of integration forty-five years ago. The fall of the iron curtain makes it now imperative for the EU to open itself for the new democratic market economies in Central and Eastern Europe. Ten of them plus Malta and Cyprus have applied for EU membership. All of them also want to join NATO. Both enlargement processes serve the same goal: To roll the Western European carpet of stability further East and South.

Enlarging the European Union

EU membership will guarantee political and economic stability in our immediate neighborhood. In 1993, the EU promised to welcome all ten Central and Eastern European states as members, if and when a clear set of criteria is fulfilled:

- Stable democratic institutions
- The rule of law
- Human rights and respect and protection of minorities
- A functioning market economy
- The capacity to cope with the competitive pressure of market forces within the Union

These countries are working hard to transform their political and economic systems to EU standards. We support them as much as we can. Germany has a logical and natural interest in incorporating its Eastern neighbors into the EU It was not to be taken for granted that France would share this view. We are all the more gratified that France shares her energies with us in this great endeavor together with all our other EU partners, just as we Germans share and support France's interest in stabilizing the Mediterranean neighborhood with a new

EU partnership program. Stability to the East and to the South are of vital importance to the EU as a whole.

The question is no longer "if" the Central and Eastern European countries will join the EU but only "when" and "how." Probably in 1998, the EU will have to decide about the modalities of the negotiations for enlargement. Should the EU start negotiating with all twelve candidates at the same time, or should we start first with a group of the most advanced countries? If the latter is followed, what will be the effects on those countries not to be admitted in the first round? Again, France and Germany are developing a common idea about how to tackle this problem. Our foreign ministries have put forward the idea of convening a "European conference" of all the parties concerned—EU member states, all candidate countries, plus the Commission. The goal would be to combine efforts for a smooth accession process.

Enlargement of the EU has not only a political dimension. Rapid economic globalization gives it also vital economic importance for Europe. In comparison to America and other centers of economic growth, Europe is losing ground. Western Europe's eighteen million jobless is an alarming symptom and Europe obviously must increase its competitiveness. Thus, the pressure for structural change in Western Europe is increasing. The economies in Central and Eastern Europe register high growth rates of approximately five percent a year. This means new markets for us, but also new competitors. This may be bitter for individual sectors, but on balance and over the medium to long term, the integration of Eastern Europe will help to increase our own competitiveness on world markets.

Enlargement will change the face of the EU. It will become a Union of up to twenty-seven member states, more heterogeneous than ever. We, therefore, need to organize more efficiently and we cannot go on simply adding new stories to the European house originally constructed for six tenants. The house will simply collapse one day. It is therefore essential to carry out a successful institutional reform prior to the accession of new members. We must get the Union into shape for enlargement. Its internal coherence must be strengthened.

Reforming the European Union

The EU member states convened in an intergovernmental conference in March 1996. The goal of the conference is to review the
Maastricht Treaty and to improve European cooperation for the new
challenges ahead of us. Again, France and Germany took the lead in
putting forward a number of suggestions to our other EU partners.
In a joint letter in December 1995, Federal Chancellor Kohl and
President Chirac outlined what in their view should be the main goals.
Recently, our Foreign Ministers met in Paris to elaborate a new paper
that specifies our joint ideas on some of the crucial questions and will
hopefully give new impetus to the conference.

I should like to highlight just two of the issues: First, and most
importantly, the European Union should in the future speak with one
voice in the international arena. Our aim is to give the Union greater
scope for action in its external relations. The foreign and security
policies of member states need to be more coherently bundled. Europe
as a whole must act more quickly, more efficiently and more visibly
in international relations. The example most often quoted in public
is the inability of the EU to contribute more successfully to the solution
of the war in the former Yugoslavia. Why was Richard Holbrooke
able to reach a breakthrough when the European Union had not
succeeded? It seems clear that we need a closer coordination of our
planning and analysis, as well as our action. France and Germany,
therefore, suggest a joint planning and analysis center which should
provide collective foreign policy analyses and options as well as steer
and manage European action.

In addition, we feel we owe Henry Kissinger an answer to his
question: "Who is Mr. Europe? Give me his telephone number!"
Understandably, the outside world finds it difficult to identify who
is speaking or acting on behalf of "Europe." Is it the presidency, the
Troika, individual states, or the Commission? Europe must not always
act together, but if it does act as "Europe," the world must understand
that this is what is being done. We, therefore, feel that one person
should be appointed to speak and act on behalf of EU foreign policy.

This person should be responsible to the Council of Ministers and carry out their instructions. I admit that France and Germany are not completely in agreement on the status of this person. While we think that he or she should be some sort of a secretary general clearly subordinate to foreign ministers, France prefers the idea of a "Monsieur PESC" (French for CFSP), with more stature.

In addition, we believe that for decision-making in foreign policy, the EU should leave the consensus principle behind as it has in many other areas of cooperation and adopt qualified majority voting in the Council. Needless to say, this is a particularly difficult step. The idea of being outvoted by others in matters of foreign policy cuts deeply into the traditional understanding of national sovereignty. But we think such a step is inevitable if the EU wants to be able to act quickly and resolutely. In the area of security policy, however, the consensus principle must remain in force for the time being. It would be unthinkable, for us as for others, that armed forces be deployed without the consent of the nation contributing the troops.

Experience in former Yugoslavia also shows that crisis prevention and peacekeeping can only be effective if foreign policy has the option of using military means. The IGC must, therefore, make progress towards developing a European military capacity. The Western European Union is the instrument. By integrating WEU into the EU, the European Union will in the future be able to field a force of its own. This could happen if the U.S. decides its interests are not involved and prefers not to engage its own forces. I am aware of American doubts about how a European defense identity would fit with NATO. Let there be no doubt: NATO remains at the core of America's and Europe's common security. Collective defense against potential aggression must remain a NATO matter. Neither do we intend to duplicate existing alliance structures. It is through NATO and by using NATO resources that we want to organize our European capabilities in the security field. The French move towards reintegration into NATO facilitates the linkage between NATO and WEU. At the NATO Council meeting in December 1996, Europeans and Americans decided on concrete steps for a more visible and independent European stance in the field of crisis prevention and peacekeeping.

Another aspect of the IGC worth mentioning is the Franco-German suggestion for a general flexibility clause. While in the past all EU member states have undertaken the same obligations in all fields, thus creating a uniform set of rules applicable to all of them alike, the Maastricht Treaty deviated from this principle. It contains some opt-out clauses as well as provisions for a faster integration of some member states in some areas. Not all EU member states will, for example, join the European Monetary Union at the same time. A step-by-step process is explicitly foreseen. Some might never qualify. Other member states have opted out from other fields, European defense for example. Not all share the same willingness for further integration. New members could bring new problems and divergences.

The slowest ship in the convoy should not prevent the others from moving forward a little faster. This is why Germany and France suggest that, in the future, member states that are able and willing to cooperate more closely should have the opportunity to do so. A flexibility clause in the treaty should make this possible. With this suggestion Germany and France want to give new dynamism to integration, not create a core Europe. Thus, we agree that no member state wishing to participate should be excluded. The EU's uniform institutional framework must remain intact. Not all our partners in the EU are enthusiastic about our idea. But we feel that in a Union with more and more members and with more diverging interests, integration can be pushed ahead only in this way.

In this context, I would like to mention European Monetary Union—perhaps the most important Franco-German initiative for Europe—before closing. While in the U.S. the dollar is legal tender for 265 million people from New York to Los Angeles, the EU alone has fourteen different currencies. It is an anachronism that Europe should have a single market, with free movement of labor, capital, goods and services, but not a common currency. Fluctuations of exchange rates cause enormous economic losses. Estimates suggest that as a consequence, hundreds of thousands of jobs have been lost and new jobs not created. The advantages of our internal market can only be fully exploited with a common currency. The European currency, the euro, thus is the logical extension of the single market.

It was natural for France and Germany, the biggest exporters in the EU, to call for a common currency. Germany has an additional interest in creating the euro: The Deutsche Mark is overburdened by serving as the second most important reserve currency of the world. Our country has to bear the brunt of any single disturbance or irritation of the international capital markets. The euro, however, must be as stable as the Deutsche Mark is today. Therefore, a number of difficult fiscal and monetary requirements have to be fulfilled. By January 1, 1999, a first group of EU countries will fix their exchange rates to each other in terms of the euro. Not all EU members will by then fulfill the strict criteria for economic stability specified in the Treaty as a precondition for entry. Even Germany and a number of other countries now have difficulty fulfilling these conditions. Since the euro is a historic chance for Europe, both France and Germany have swallowed the bitter pill of reducing their budget deficits in order to comply with the requirements of the euro.

I am convinced that in 1999, Europe will have the common currency. One thing is clear: Germany and France must belong to this core monetary group. The European currency will over time change international capital markets. The U.S. dollar will also feel the effects. My advice to America is: familiarize yourselves with the idea of a strong and stable European currency.

Former French Foreign Minister Hervé de Charette recently said: "La monnaie, c'est bien entendu un projet politique." I could not agree more. The common currency will make European integration irreversible. It will strengthen European cohesion. It will lead us one big step further toward the great Franco-German vision of the economic and political Union of Europe, a Europe that will be a strong partner for America.

Notes

[1] Warren Christopher, "A New Atlantic Community for the 21st Century," Speech, September 6, 1996, Stuttgart, Germany.

[2] Martin Gilbert, *Winston S. Churchill*, vol. 8, pp. 265–66.

FRENCH AND GERMAN APPROACHES TO ORGANIZING EUROPE'S FUTURE SECURITY AND DEFENSE: A FRENCH PERSPECTIVE

François Heisbourg

Introduction: The Legacy of *Réconciliation Franco-Allemande*

The special relationship between France and Germany rests on the lessons drawn in both countries from the shared experience of war and defeat. The wars are those of 1870–71, 1914–18 and 1939–45. In and of themselves, such conflicts would not create any particular feeling of togetherness, rather the opposite. Thus, the lack of positive emotion in the German-British relationship since 1945 stands in contrast to the French-German post-war *rapprochement*. What probably provided the cement to the Franco-German couple is the extreme trauma of utter defeat both countries underwent in 1940 and 1945, respectively. Each was faced with complete humiliation and near annihilation as functioning polities before undergoing a process of back-from-the-brink redemption. France unexpectedly emerged as a victor at the end of the war thanks to a combination of circumstances. France benefited from the constant political and military support of the United Kingdom, the exceptional role of Charles de Gaulle, the eventual formation of a vigorous resistance movement, and the crucial military assistance of the United States and other allies. As for occupied Germany, it was able to embark on the path of democratization under the far-sighted leadership and with the generous support of the United States. Both France and Germany successfully rebuilt their shattered economies, not least with the help of the Marshall Plan.

In the immediate aftermath of the Axis defeat in 1945, an impoverished France imposed a tough regime in its allotted occupation zone in Germany (essentially the Saarland, the Palatinate and much of Baden-Württemberg). French diplomacy was actively seeking to annex the left bank of the Rhine, to internationalize the Ruhr, and to avoid the reemergence of a united Germany. On the face of it, little in the French approach had changed from the counterproductive vindictiveness of the years following Germany's defeat in 1918. Yet, as early as 1946, a deliberate effort was made by private individuals—including French survivors of Dachau such as Edmond Michelet and Joseph Rovan—and by the occupation authorities to promote reconciliation through cultural and political cooperation. These seeds, which fell on increasingly fertile ground, were the origins of the state-to-state and people-to-people cooperation that would later blossom. By 1952, much of the French body politic had accepted the idea of a rapprochement to the extent of the ill-fated proposal for a European Defense Community (EDC), in which Germany was to rearm as part of a European Army under NATO. The French Parliament's failure to ratify the EDC in August 1954 was not out of fear of Germany, but out of concern about France's sovereignty, given that most of the French army was to come under the control of a supranational body akin to today's European Commission. Within the following year France, along with the other allies, had approved Germany's entry into the WEU and NATO. Cold War strategic realities naturally played a considerable part in this respect.

In January and November 1957, the French and the German Defense Ministers (Jacques Chaban-Delmas and Franz-Josef Strauss) concluded, along with their Italian colleague, a set of broad-ranging secret military agreements, which provided *inter alia* for cooperation on ballistic missiles and nuclear weapons.[1] This went further than the political traffic could bear. Indeed, one of de Gaulle's first decisions during his tenure as Prime Minister in June 1958 was to suspend this secret agreement, the specific contents of which became known only some thirty-five years later. Still, the whole episode gives some idea of the depth and speed of the rapprochement, even in the most sensitive areas.

At the same time, a latent fear of Germany's resurgence continued to color France's approach to Germany.[2] De Gaulle excluded Germany from his stillborn initiative of September 1958 to set up a Franco-British-American *directoire* to steer NATO policy. And it was not until 1985 that France acquiesced to the lifting of the ultimate restrictions on Germany's right to produce certain types of conventional weapons (long-range missiles in particular) under the terms of Germany's admission into the WEU in 1954.

However, that a terrible past would recur has acted not as a brake, but as an engine of Franco-German cooperation. It was a cement, not a solvent, of the relationship. This paradox can only be explained if one takes into account the vivid emotions created by the experience of war and defeat, i.e., the couple's psychological basis. But because it is tied to memory, it is also vulnerable to the passage of time, a consideration that will be elaborated further. Nevertheless, so far whenever there has been a risk of crisis in French-German relations—as at the time of rearmament (1952–55) or during reunification (1990–91)—the joint reflex has been to hold each other more tightly, since a close embrace makes a parting of ways more difficult.

From "Paris *or* Washington?" to "Paris *and* Washington"

During most of the Cold War, the Franco-German defense and security relationship was bedeviled by the divergence of views on the role of the United States and NATO. For Gaullist France, the vision was one of strategic independence vis-à-vis the U.S., as exemplified by France's nuclear stance, her withdrawal from NATO's integrated military command structure, and the departure of American and Canadian forces from France. In 1963, Bonn was invited to share this vision, but the West German attitude was, of course, rather different. Indeed, NATO's new doctrine of Forward Defense against Warsaw Pact forces poised on the Elbe reinforced alignment with Washington, discouraging initiatives such as the one made by Franz-Josef Strauss in the nuclear arena in 1957-58. Furthermore, the Federal Republic's armed forces embraced a degree of integration within NATO exceeding that of any other major member. Postwar Germany never attempted to recreate a General Staff. Integrated NATO in general, and CINCENT (Commander-in-Chief Central Europe)[3] in particular, emerged as proxies for a national defense staff. This had the strategic advantage of enhancing NATO's military cohesion in the key Central European theater and the political benefit of avoiding an uncomfortable return to a past marked by the existence of an assertive command structure. If anything, France's withdrawal in 1966 emphasized this trend, since one of the immediate effects was that CINCENT, hitherto a French General, was entrusted to a West German General.

The Bedrock of "Construction Européenne" and the Franco-German Grand Bargain

On the face of it, such divergence of strategic perspective, reinforced by France's independent nuclear policy, was hardly conducive to what was later portrayed as a Franco-German alliance within the Alliance. Indeed, the positive weight of emotions could probably not have outweighed such a divisive issue, had there not been a much broader base to the relationship. From the early 1950s onward, this base was provided not simply by the existence of specific objective interests, however significant they may have been (such as the fact that the two countries were then and are now each other's main trading partners). Rather, from the early fifties onward there was an early political understanding between France and Germany that they needed each other in order to shape Western Europe's economic and political order. Initially, Germany needed France more than France needed Germany, with the balance shifting over the years. On its own, neither could have decisively molded the European Community.

The Franco-German connection was all the more readily established and consolidated because the United Kingdom deliberately refused *ab initio* to join the European Coal and Steel Community, the EDC,[4] Euratom, or the European Economic Community. By the time London measured the scale of its blunder (1963), the Franco-German bond was sealed, and it has never ceased to operate as the primary force in the process of European construction. The shared interest and the benefits of German-French *Zusammenarbeit* sufficed to enable the two countries to surmount their serious differences over the eventual endpoint of European construction: Adenauer's vision of a federalist Europe was hardly identical to de Gaulle's *Europe des Patries,* as exemplified by the Fouché Plan in the early 1960s. This difference remains present to this day. However, long-term objectives did not and still do not prevent Bonn and Paris from agreeing to mutually acceptable interim steps. This grand bargain on the economic, political, and, to a large extent, social dimensions of the Western European order helped circumscribe and circumvent the difficulties created by different strategic outlooks and rhetoric.

1963–82: Accommodating Strategic Divergence

The first half of 1963 was to define the manner in which France and Germany were to accommodate their differing NATO-Anschauungen during the following two decades. January 1963 witnessed the signing of the Elysée Treaty, which established *inter alia* a full strategic partnership between France and Germany. The language of the Treaty[5] and the consultative machinery it set out to create appeared in the eyes of many to accomplish France's desire to see Bonn choose "Paris rather than Washington." This interpretation was no doubt excessive, since it is not unnatural that a bilateral treaty should hardly mention third countries or multilateral organizations. However, this perception colored the reaction of a majority of the members of the *Bundestag* when the agreement came up for ratification in June 1963. The preliminary declaration which was nailed onto the Treaty in the ratification process in Bonn aimed to correct this impression. In doing so, the *Bundestag* clearly chose "Washington rather than Paris," which in turn upset the French. As a result, the politico-military consultative machinery was not set up.

Bilateral defense cooperation—albeit limited by the impossibility of striking a broader strategic compromise—did develop, however. Armaments cooperation took off in a fairly big way, both as a result of the Treaty and as a spin-off from the conventional arms provisions of the 1957 Chaban-Strauss agreement. Franco-German transport aircraft (Transall), close air-support and trainer aircraft (Alphajet), anti-tank missiles (Hot, Milan), and air defense systems (Roland) were some of the more prominent results of the military-industrial cooperation. All are still in service today. Tight technical and defense-industrial bonds were generated in the process, notably between firms such as Aerospatiale and DASA,[6] and between defense research establishments. Part of this was the unforeseen consequence of the assimilation of German technicians captured or enrolled by the French in 1945–46 into French establishments—a French equivalent of America's "Paper Clip" operation—which played a major, albeit rarely acknowledged role in the postwar development of France's defense and space industries. Close relations were established at the local level between the French forces in Germany (Deuxième Corps d'Armée) and the German authorities. However, this remained a low-key affair. France's forces in Germany were not part of NATO's *forward defense*— politically and strategically essential to the FRG—and, in case war broke out, they would remain confined west of the so-called RDM line running from Rotterdam to Munich via Dortmund. Furthermore, French-NATO contingency planning was not by definition a Franco-German affair, even if the Valentin-Ferber agreements of 1974 (named after the then-commanders of the French First Army and NATO's CINCENT) were signed by a Frenchman and a German.

Nuclear matters played an ambivalent role. On the one hand, they served—much as was the case for U.S. nuclear weapons in Europe—as an irritant in the relationship. The West Germans did not relish the prospect of becoming a nuclear battlefield for French Pluton short-range missiles vying with U.S. *Lance* and Soviet *Scuds*. However, the irritation remained secondary in comparison to the major rows surrounding the U.S. neutron bomb controversy in the mid-1970s, or NATO's double-track decision in 1979–83. The numbers simply were not the same and, unlike U.S. nukes, in peacetime France's nuclear weapons remained deployed within France. At the same time, the German government appreciated the contribution which France's nuclear force provided to the Alliance's deterrent posture, as evinced in NATO's Ottawa declaration of June 1974.[7]

The overall strategic divisions remained unreconciled, and only one major and unsuccessful attempt was made in 1975 to bring them closer. That year, the French Chief of Defense Staff, Général Méry, suggested that a brigade-sized French force from the First Army should be tasked to operate East of the RDM line in case of conflict. This was accompanied by a speech by President Giscard d'Estaing alluding to the possibility of *sanctuarisation élargie*, i.e., that French nuclear forces would be brandished not only in defense of French territory strictly defined *(le sanctuaire)*, but also to the benefit of neighboring territory. Virulent reactions by the Neo-Gaullists of the RPR forced a rapid backtracking, and no more was heard until after the next change of President in 1981.

Towards a "Bündnis im Bündnis": The Turning Point of 1982

The first months of the Mitterrand presidency saw little substantial change in French-German relations. If anything the relationship suffered from a lack of empathy between the new French President and Chancellor Schmidt. This contrasted with the exceptionally close rapport established previously between the German Chancellor and President Giscard d'Estaing. Furthermore, as is often the case in the early stages of a new French administration, there was some temptation to balance the Franco-German couple with greater closeness between Paris and London. Such was the case after President Pompidou's election in 1969, in 1993 when Mr. Balladur became Prime Minister and in 1995 after Mr. Chirac's election to the presidency. Such attempts, even when accompanied by a significant degree of sustained British responsiveness (which has only happened once when Prime Minister Heath was President Pompidou's interlocutor) do not in themselves represent an alternative to the primacy of the Franco-

German bilateral relationship; but they can affect the climate between Paris and Bonn.

After a period of initial hesitancy, however, things began to change. The strong support that President Mitterrand gave to NATO's "double track decision" of December 1979, concerning the deployment of Pershing II and ground-based cruise missiles, helped to face down the Soviet challenge to European and Atlantic security and resolve the Euro-missile crisis. In March 1982, the Defense and Foreign Ministers of the two countries decided that they should meet regularly before the semestrial French-German summit meetings to discuss defense and security affairs. The implementation of this plan was delayed by the subsequent political turmoil which led to the ousting of Chancellor Schmidt, disavowed by his own party for his strong stance on the Euro-missile issue.

When Chancellor Kohl came into office in October 1982—with Herr Genscher remaining in charge of the Foreign Ministry—there was a strong and practically immediate meeting of minds between the new Chancellor and the French President. This development was replicated between the French Minister of Defense, Monsieur Hernu, and his new German colleague, Herr Wörner, who was considerably more robust on the Euro-missile issue than his SPD predecessor, Herr Apel, and more strongly inclined towards French-German cooperation. The new dynamic led not only to the first intimate and successful meeting of the Foreign and Defense Ministers (each assisted by only one note taker) in Bonn, but to the decision of October 1982 to implement, de facto, the defense strategy provisions of the Elysée Treaty. Thus was born the Committee on Security and Defense, which first met in Paris on December 7, 1982. Its restricted and well-tailored composition[8] made for easy, frequent, and effective cooperation for the rest of the eighties. Three subgroups were set up: politico-strategic; military cooperation; and armaments cooperation. Plenary meetings took place once every three or four months.

At the rhetorical level, Chancellor Kohl captured the spirit of the change at the Franco-German Summit of December 1982. The choice, he said, was not "Paris *or* Washington, but Paris *and* Washington." A major psychological hurdle had been passed by both countries, even though the practical differences in defense policy, strategy and force posture remained. President Mitterrand's landmark speech to the Bundestag on January 22, 1983, strongly supporting the German government's efforts to secure the deployment of the American Pershing IIs and GLCMs against widespread popular opposition, was the spectacular manifestation of this process.

The following years witnessed a burgeoning of initiatives flowing from the breakthrough of 1982. Paris eliminated its references to Germany as a mere *glacis* of Fortress France and dropped its language about France's vital interests being limited to French territory. The new emphasis from 1984 onward was placed on commonality of destiny. Changes in nuclear rhetoric and force posture deemphasized the geographical definition of France's vital interests as limited solely to her territory. Tactical nuclear missiles were placed under the operational control of the Chief of the French Defense Staff rather than at lower levels. Finally, joint military maneuvers (notably *"Kecker Spatz/ Moineau Hardi"*) were held in 1985 in the Danube area, well forward of the RDM line.

The decision in June 1987 to establish a joint Franco-German military unit at the brigade level was a symbolic high point of this process in the pre-reunification period, as was the upgrading of the Commission on Security and Defense, which had hitherto been chaired by the Foreign and Defense Ministers. A Defense and Security Council, presided over by the German Chancellor and the French President, was established in place of the former Committee and endowed with a permanent secretariat. Unfortunately, as subsequent events were to demonstrate, what the new body gained in prestige and visibility, it lost in effectiveness as a conduit for in-depth and upstream consultation. The extraordinary degree of trust and respect existing between Chancellor Kohl and President Mitterrand—two men brought together by the importance they both gave to the lessons of history and their resulting European convictions—was no doubt a major element in the equation. The high emotions as they walked hand-in-hand to commemorate the great slaughter at Verdun, more than outweighed the continuing differences in NATO participation and nuclear status.

Post–Cold War Trends

The Impact of Reunification

The initial French response to the events taking place in Germany in the last weeks of 1989 can be characterized as a combination of intellectual lucidity and political short-sightedness. President Mitterrand, in particular, understood what was going on. Indeed, the French—a people with a strong sense of nation—were not slow in assuming that the Germans would seize the opportunity to restore their own undivided nationhood. The French were not prone to believe in the long term viability of an ideological-strategic artifact such as the GDR. At the same time, the French President, and indeed most of the French body politic, did not like what they saw. While recognizing the inevitability of the process, the Elysée appeared to want to slow it down, and channel it. President Mitterrand's attempt to enlist President Gorbachev in this enterprise (the Kiev meeting) and his subsequent ill-advised trip to the GDR in December 1989 were signs of this.

In addition, there was a tendency to overestimate Soviet resistance to reunification. Worse, the appearance of French-Polish connivance on the Oder-Neisse border issue inflamed relations between Paris and Bonn in the opening months of 1990. Furthermore, this policy was conducted against the backdrop of widespread French fears that a reunited Germany would become a hegemon in Europe, that *l'Allemagne européenne* would be replaced by *l'Europe allemande*. In effect, France grudgingly followed the flow of events which it could not prevent. According to the most recent and authoritative accounts, President Mitterrand was subsequently to acknowledge that he had missed the opportunity of seizing the historical moment.[9]

Although this performance stands in contrast to the outstanding U.S. record during this period, France's policy did not substantially upset French-German relations. The reason was that France and Germany continued to share a common interest in jointly shaping the future of the European Community. In a sense, Chancellor Kohl and President Mitterrand moved away from a potentially risky bilateral crisis by launching a multilateral initiative. In Spring 1990, they effectively initiated the process which led to the Maastricht Treaty and the creation of the European Union. To avoid "l'Europe allemande," France decided to move Europe forward with Germany in a manner considered to be protective of French interests. Similarly, a uniting Germany found in the creation of a closer European Union a way to avoid a re-nationalization of its foreign and security policy, a prospect which it viewed with extreme apprehension, given the record of the previous period of German unity from 1871 to 1945. Chancellor Kohl's insistence that the entirety of a united Germany be a fully fledged member of NATO helped to avoid re-nationalization in the area of defense policy. For France and Germany, the European foundation had once again served its purpose. By contrast, from 1989 onward the United Kingdom found its relationship with Germany and the E.C. stuck in a dead-end.

In the area of security and defense, reunification was also accompanied by a push for greater Europeanization. France and Germany pressed hard for the inclusion of machinery for an EU Common Foreign and Security Policy (CFSP) in the Maastricht Treaty of December 1991. This included the long term prospect of a common defense policy. Similarly, the Western European Union (WEU) was strongly supported as the kernel of a European defense and security identity; language about the WEU being the "European pillar of NATO" as well as the "military arm of Europe" made it possible for Germany not to choose between "Paris and Washington." Last but not least, Paris and Bonn announced in October 1992 the establishment of an integrated army corps, the Eurocorps. Subsequently joined by Spain, Belgium and Luxembourg, this 50,000 soldier unit became operational on December 1, 1995.

Thus, out of the bilateral difficulties linked to reunification arose new Franco-German initiatives. Indeed, subsequent contentious episodes—most notably the German unilateral decision to recognize Croatia in December 1991—were considered as further proof of the need for tighter integration.

The Effects of Post–Cold War Strategic and Military Reform

Reunification was one of the major features at the end of the Cold War; the disappearance of the Warsaw Pact and of the Soviet Union was another. Together, they brought to an end the massive military threat present in the heart of Europe. This has had both short-term and long-term effects on the French-German relationship, possibly of greater importance than the mechanical fact that the Federal Republic of Germany has absorbed an additional sixteeen million inhabitants and 108,000 square kilometers of real estate; an area blighted by over forty years of collectivism and half a century of dictatorship.

The immediate impact of the evaporation of the Soviet threat was to provoke a major realignment of the currencies of power in Europe. During the Cold War, the hard currency of military power weighed in France's favor. The possession of an independent nuclear deterrent, combined with forces deployed in Germany, gave France a self-confidence and an influence which more than made up for the greater economic strength and financial stability of West Germany.

The metaphor of Germany as an economic giant and political dwarf was no doubt overstated. There was, however, an element of truth about the statement that the Cold War French-German relationship was an *équilibre des déséquilibres*—an overall balance of sectional imbalances, that eventually were compensating. In any event, after 1990 the "exchange rate" of nukes collapsed, while that of the Deutsche Mark and the Bundesbank soared. This was promptly recognized in France, and much of the energy behind the policy of the *franc fort* has come from this recognition. In contrast to the succession of devaluations vis-à-vis the Deutsche Mark between 1981 and 1986, the nineties have been characterized by the Franc acquiring the stability of the mark. French worries about a dominant German economy were attenuated by the realization that the new Länder would represent a long-term burden on Germany's finances—with recessionary knock-on effects in Europe as interest rates rose in response to Germany's international borrowing requirements—and that Germany's social and economic rigidities were hardly less daunting than those prevalent in France. The fact remained, and remains, that the reduced importance of military power has introduced a new element of lopsidedness in the French-German couple.

The longer-term consequences provoked by the end of the Cold War flow from the manner in which France and Germany have responded in strategic and military terms to the new set of circumstances. During the first half of the nineties, no significant new discrepancy emerged between the policies of France and Germany in these areas. On the other hand, budgetary trends were no doubt different: Federal Germany's defense spending fell by approximately a third between 1989 and 1995, and military manpower dropped from 490,000 to 340,000; in France, the corresponding figures were approximately ten percent spending reductions and 48,000 fewer military personnel (mostly conscripts). However, this was not accompanied by a new divergence of strategy between the two countries. Indeed, a number of major elements of convergence emerged during this period.

- Germany, which had found it extraordinarily difficult to fulfill its NATO obligations during the Gulf War (e.g., the debate about deployment of German planes assigned to SHAPE's allied mobile force in Turkey), subsequently pursued a careful and deliberate policy of increasing its ability to operate militarily with its allies outside the NATO area. A military medical team in Cambodia (1992) and Blue Helmets in a non-combat position in Mogadishu (1993) were the forerunners. In July 1994, the Constitutional Court in Karlsruhe had interpreted the German constitution as allowing participation in allied operations approved by the Bundestag. Luftwaffe Tornados were deployed in Italy in 1994; they flew electronic warfare missions as part of Operation Deliberate Force during August and September 1995. In December 1995, Bundeswehr troops were based in Croatia as part of IFOR, the next step being the dispatch of combat troops to Bosnia as part of the successor force to IFOR. Thus, Germany's ability and readiness to participate in coalition operations, while still remaining short of British and French practice, has become much greater, reducing one of the major discrepancies between France's and Germany's defense policy and posture. The establishment of a German rapid deployment force (KRK—Krisen Reaktionskräfte) will reinforce the convergence.

• France gradually reduced, and eventually eliminated, those elements of its nuclear force posture which created the most problems for German public opinion. Pluton short-range missiles (equivalent to U.S. Lance) were decommissioned in the early nineties. Their putative successors, Hades, were produced in small numbers without being deployed operationally. Furthermore, they were dismantled in 1996.

• France and Germany tentatively agreed to work together on military surveillance satellites, strategic intelligence being generally recognized as a top post–Cold War priority. In December 1995, President Chirac and Chancellor Kohl sealed the political deal. Germany would join in the production of the Helios II optical reconnaissance satellite under French prime contractorship. Due to enter service in 2001, this project is a follow-on to the French-Italian-Spanish Helios I, operational since July 1995. Meanwhile, France would participate in the future Horus military radar satellite under German prime-contractorship. This Franco-German cooperation was achieved in the face of intense high-level pressure from all relevant U.S. agencies and was an area in which Bonn had been entirely in Washington's hands. The Americans clearly have not appreciated the German quest for a link with Paris in such a key area.

If one adds the establishment of the Eurocorps, the first steps of defense reforms were overall positive. Indeed, there is a remarkable degree of convergence in the analysis and policies laid out in the first post–Cold War French and German White Papers, both published in 1994. However, this comparatively incremental process took a sudden and spectacular twist from the end of 1995 onward. As is often the case in French history, long periods of *immobilisme* are followed by intense and across-the-board bursts of reform, if not outright revolution. Whereas, other Alliance partners had initiated adaptation to changing strategic circumstances earlier on, and in a more-or-less sequential fashion, in France, reforms have been delayed beyond reason, and now all is happening at the same time:

• During the second half of 1995, the defense budget took a sharp dive, with procurement expenditure dropping suddenly by around twenty percent within a six-month period.

• In December 1995, France announced its decision to return to NATO's Military Committee with a view to participating in the renovation and Europeanization of the Alliance's integrated structure. Thus, France acknowledged that NATO was the only credible multilateral military institution in Europe and that the WEU could not perform this role.

• In February 1996, the French President outlined plans for the following, *inter alia:*
   —a reduction of the armed forces from 500,000 to 350,000 uniformed personnel, with a strong emphasis on professionalization and force projection, inferring that obligatory military service would disappear;
   —across-the-board cuts in ongoing and prospective armaments programs, including those conducted in a French-German framework;
   —a massive restructuring of the defense industry, with the merger of Dassault and Aerospatiale, and the privatization of Thomson.

• In May 1996, the principle of conscription was formally abandoned by the President, with an all-volunteer force to be phased in over a maximum of six years, and Mr. Chirac announced in July that the draft would cease to apply to new age cohorts from January 1997 onwards—only draftees on deferral were to be inducted after that date.

French developments related to NATO were obviously welcomed by Germany. But overall, the initial official reaction to the other elements of defense reform were vigorously negative. The abandonment of the draft, the emphasis on force projection and the sharp and unexpected reduction of the joint armaments program, the apparent French-centeredness of the restructuring of the defense industry all drew widely hostile reactions. The German Defense Minister, Volker Rühe, went on record condemning France's attempt to transform the Eurocorps into a new "Afrikakorps." This was an extreme example on a broad spectrum of negative responses. One of the more widespread arguments was that France, by reducing her forces, would somehow leave Germany saddled with responsibility for Europe's territorial defense. Although it is not difficult to demonstrate that the French reforms (if implemented as stated) will do nothing of the sort, this impression reflected Germany's perception that France was exceedingly focused on out-of-Europe contingencies. These reactions were reinforced and entrenched by two factors.

First, French-German consultations prior to President Chirac's announcements had not been up to the standards of the eighties. Although communication on some of these issues had been good at the President-to-Chancellor level, this was far from being the case elsewhere. No prior notice was given of the approximate scope of reductions affecting French-German programs (notably the NH 90 transport helicopter, the Tiger combat helicopter, the Brevel battlefield drone, the future military transport aircraft, the MEADS extended air defense system). Furthermore, the Germans can be excused for feeling that they had been misled about conscription. Whereas President Chirac was in favor of an all-volunteer force, the French Defense Ministry was still expecting, on the eve of the President's announcement, that some form of conscription would be maintained; this impression was transmitted to the German Defense Ministry as late as February 20, just two days beforehand. Given the parlous state of military service in Germany—with one out of two draftees opting for conscientious objection—such an impression was all too eagerly received by German officials eager to prevent the abandonment of the draft in their own country. The subsequent disappointment was commensurate with the previous raising of expectations. On this score, it must be said that consultation was probably lacking between the two banks of the Seine, just as much as between the two sides of the Rhine.

The breakdown in consultation was widespread. Thus, the secretariat of the joint Defense and Security Council was not in the loop. The arrival of a new team in Paris after the presidential elections in May 1995 and the initial period of hesitation between French-British and French-German relations were no doubt contributing factors. However, this lack of communication in comparison to previous years may also be an indication of the potential impact of the change of generations (see last section).

The second major aggravating factor was the fortuitous discrepancy in timing between French and German budget decisions. The German Defense Ministry, after five years of spending cuts, was facing a prospective new onslaught from the Finance Ministry in the first months of 1996. The internationally cooperative nature of much of Germany's armaments spending was to be used as a major argument by the Defense Ministry in resisting new cuts in the defense procurement budget. Alas, the unilateral French decisions of February and May 1996 pulled that carpet from under Herr Rühe's feet. This, in turn, created the risk of a vicious circle: subsequent German defense cuts in July 1996 affect French-German programs, which could force the French to cut further, and so on.

It took a series of impromptu as well as normal meetings—between the French President and the German Chancellor, and between the Defense Ministers—to confine the resulting damage. As the French case for the military reforms is basically sound, it can be hoped that reconvergence will ensue. Budget cuts were inevitable in France, as they have been in Germany. In addition, France's defense industry, after restructuring, will not be nearly as concentrated and national as Germany's, with its one overwhelming defense contractor, Daimler-Benz Aerospace. Conscription is probably becoming as unworkable in Germany as it had become in France. Even with 350,000 uniformed personnel, France will still have a larger military than Germany. Force projection is becoming a priority in Germany, as well as in France. Finally, France, Germany and the U.K. have been working hand-in-glove on the reform of NATO. In particular, Bonn, Paris and London responded vigorously and successfully against U.S. attempts to water down a previously negotiated agreement on Combined Joint Task Forces before NATO's Berlin Summit in June 1996.

In the meantime, no doubt, the overall French-German relationship is sufficiently robust to circumscribe and accommodate the very substantial difficulties created by France's defense reform and the German reactions. Nevertheless, the dispute over defense policy was indicative of a new and not entirely reassuring development in French-German relations. The question is whether this was a taste of things to come or simply a virulent, but isolated, tiff.

Prospects: Renationalization or Europeanization?

Three interlinked sets of developments will determine whether the French-German engine in the field of security and defense can continue to operate successfully and, if so, how: 1) the consequences of the moves toward the single currency; 2) the management of EU and NATO enlargements; and 3) generational changes.

European Integration: The Consequences of a Single Currency

As in previous decades, the future security and defense relationship between France and Germany will depend on the evolution of the broader compact on European affairs. As things stand, this appears to be in good shape. There was some doubt during the early months of the Chirac presidency, marked both by apparent ambiguity on the single currency and by heavy flirtation with London. Since October 25, 1995, when President Chirac clearly threw his weight behind the achievement of Economic and Monetary Union (EMU), there is no doubt about the direction and single-mindedness of French policy. Convergence has been facilitated by the fact that the Germans have discovered that it will be every bit as difficult for them to achieve the Maastricht Treaty criteria for EMU as it will be for France. Thus united by an identical and equally demanding challenge, the two partners are committed to the single currency; together they are the force which is leading much of the European Union in that same direction. If EMU occurs, the security and defense consequences will be major, albeit indirect in nature: the corresponding broad vision of France and Germany will be one of further European integration and that will rebound on politico-military affairs. At the budget level, one should expect the two countries to harmonize their defense planning, and, with the establishment of the long-discussed joint armaments agency, to integrate a substantial share of their defense procurement processes. This should help avoid a repetition of the unfortunate consequences of differing budget and planning timetables. As EMU succeeds, steps toward greater political union may give substance to CFSP. French-German caucusing, already intense in the current review of NATO's command structure, will be at the heart of a European Defense and Security Identity, with the possibility of the British becoming part of a triangle.

Such developments may occur, provided EMU happens. The real question is whether the political and social traffic, notably in France, will bear the increasingly tough disciplines implied by the move to the single currency. Those disciplines would have been necessary independently of EMU, but, for better or worse, today they are attributed to the attempt to establish a single currency. A "nervous breakdown" in a society wracked by unemployment and deepening defiance vis-à-vis the "system" (to use a Le Pen word reminiscent of Nazi vocabulary about the Weimar Republic) cannot be excluded, even if this is on balance an unlikely scenario. Although such an eventuality in itself would not necessarily prevent defense and security cooperation, the consequent crisis of confidence and the absence of a common European goal would make further progress highly unlikely. The difficult quest for a European security and defense identity would become impossible.

Dilution? The Management of EU and NATO Enlargements

Although this author was not in favor of NATO enlargement on a stand alone basis, it has now become inevitable, as is also the case for the more desirable expansion of the EU. The only question is how many countries will join and when, with the widespread assumption that the Czech Republic, Hungary, Poland and Slovenia may be in the first round for both NATO and the EU. This prospect raises two sets of issues for the French-German security and defense relationship.

First, to what extent can France and Germany together serve as the engine for a rather longer European and Euro-Atlantic train? The core country concept appears to be viable and the Franco-German couple functions as the engine. In the case of security and defense, the core is already exceedingly broad: ten EU countries belong to the WEU, the remaining five have associate or observer status in that organization, and eleven are members of NATO. The future members of the EU will probably also become members of NATO and the WEU.

Therefore, the Franco-German couple will have to engage in coalition building to ensure the primacy of its initiatives. The subsidiary question then becomes one of the permanent nature of some of the coalition building, in particular, whether the French-German grouping will become a threesome with the U.K. being equally and permanently part of it. Since the U.K.'s military posture and practice is closer to that of France than to that of Germany (NATO status notwithstanding), this would appear to be a logical development. It is probably also the best way to mitigate the diluting effects of EU and NATO enlargement. However, it can only work if the U.K. shares to a substantial degree not only the French-German vision of Europe's defense and security identity, but also their attitude vis-à-vis integration in general. The latter is not presently the case.

Second, to what degree will enlargement drive French and German strategy in opposite directions? "Directions" here has a dual meaning. In one sense, this question is about France looking "South," and Germany looking "East." This is not a new situation, but having new central European members in the EU and NATO will accentuate the divide. France, in the absence of a balancing enlargement to the South (Malta and Cyprus as prospective members are not in the same league as Poland or Hungary), may find this uncomfortable. This line of reasoning is easily overstated. In practice, the main challenges to security and defense lie in directions which are not clearly Germany's East or France's South. Where are the Balkans? Where are Turkey, Iraq and the Gulf? Even the apparent exceptions (e.g., Algeria, which is clearly South) are not clear cut: Tripoli and Algiers lie closer to Munich than to Lille. In any case, none of these places poses as clear a threat of polarization of strategic relations as that great threat in the East, the USSR. If France and Germany could reconcile their "East" and "South" outlooks during the Cold War, they should be able to do so now in the new, depolarized strategic landscape, even if no U.S. hegemon points the way.

Differing directions can also mean inside or outside of Europe. This may be the more relevant divide. The German fear of being left with the burden of territorial defense while France would project forces from Rwanda to Cambodia was unreal, but it did correspond to a real question: should the Europeans have a low-profile external intervention policy, or should the interventionist practice of the U.S., France and the U.K. from 1990 to 1995 (Gulf, Kurdistan, Somalia, Bosnia) become the model for more of the same? Even if current French and German defense planning and doctrine assume the latter, the issue is probably not closed, given German reactions to the French defense reforms and the fact that the success of interventionism remains open to question. Saddam Hussein, the Aideed family, Radovan Karadzic and Slobodan Milosevic were all still in power at the time of writing. There is nothing inevitable about this issue becoming a serious source of Franco-German divergence. It is entirely possible that France, for budgetary and effectiveness reasons, will scale down its external posture, while Germany increases its political ability and readiness to participate in coalition operations. The two national processes may be converging.

Indeed, the real divergences may place reluctant Europeans at odds with cantankerous Americans. Today, there appears to be no serious French-German difference of view on the direction of NATO reform or on the desirability of having the U.S. remain present and active in European security affairs. There are, however, increasingly shared Franco-German doubts about the manner in which the U.S. combines domestic and foreign policy in the absence of an overriding external threat: the Helms-Burton and the D'Amato legislation exemplify this. Nor are these doubts confined to the French-German couple.

Generational Changes

All of the above must be viewed against the backdrop of changing generations. The good news is that French-German reconciliation is considered as a given in both countries—clearly borne out in opinion polls and at the anecdotal level. The bad news is exactly the same: the relationship is taken for granted. No longer infused with passion, the marriage may be growing stale.

One of the consistent traits of the relationship has been the importance of personalities: Adenauer-de Gaulle, Schmidt-Giscard, Kohl-Mitterrand. But to be sustained, such a relationship also has to be broad-based with continuous contact at all levels of the civil and military services (to the point of having job exchanges of civil servants), widespread twinning of cities, youth exchanges, etc.

The future is not clear on these various fronts. How European and Franco-German will Chancellor Kohl's successor be? What effect will the move of the German capital from Bonn to Berlin have on the outlook of German policy makers, a recurring worry in French circles? Can complicity at the working level thrive against a background of general public indifference?

In the same way that the U.S.-U.K. special relationship was a product of the Second World War, so the French-German couple found its relationship in the wake of major historical trauma. As that trauma fades into the background, the couple may drift apart without even realizing it (and the parallel with the U.S.-U.K. relationship probably does apply here, too).

In security and defense terms, this should not lead to anything ominous. Indifference is not antagonism. Nor should Germany's gradual, careful, and tentative return to the overt definition of a national interest create anxiety. The existence of an overt (to use an understatement) French sense of national interest has not prevented the French-German *rapprochement.*

What may help overcome the effects of the passage of time is the continued existence of an ongoing European integration process. Hence, the importance of the single currency as a means of providing a vested, shared French-German interest in shaping that process. This applies even if the British move closer to the "heart of Europe." It also applies to the fullest measure in the field of defense and security cooperation. Without the European dimension, the French-German relationship would be little different from other bilateral relationships between European countries. Certainly military cooperation would be comparatively less important in the overall Franco-German relationship than it has been during the first post–Cold War years.

Notes

[1] See G.H. Soutou, "Les accords de 1957 et 1958: vers une communauté stratégique et nucléaire entre la France, l'Allemagne et l'Italie," *La France et l'Atome,* (Bruxelles: Bruylant, 1994).

[2] A feeling strong elsewhere in Europe at the time. See, for instance, A. Horne, *Return to Power: A Report on the New Germany,* (New York: Praeger, 1956).

[3] Based in the Netherlands and encompassing practically all of West Germany in his theater of operations. Schleswig-Holstein came under CINCNORTH under certain contingencies.

[4] Although a supporter of the European Defense Community, London refused to sign on to the treaty, a factor that helped precipitate its demise in 1954.

[5] ". . . sur le plan de la stratégie et de la structure, les deux pays s'attacheront à rapprocher leurs doctrines en vue d'aboutir à des conceptions communes." Traité sur la coopération franco-allemande, 22 janvier 1963, part II (b), "Defense."

[6] As they are known today.

[7] See § 6 of the declaration, concerning French and British nuclear forces: ". . . forces nucléaires en mesure de jouer un rôle dis-suasif propre contribuant au reforcement global de la dissuasion de l'Alliance."

[8] A total of about a dozen senior civilian defense advisors, diplomats, and general officers.

[9] See H. Védrine, *Les Mondes de François Mitterrand* (Paris: Fayard, 1996), pp. 455-456, and M. Favier and M. Martin Rolland, *La Décennie Mitterrand 3,* (Paris: Seuil, 1996).

DEUX RÊVES DANS UN SEUL LIT: FRANCO-GERMAN SECURITY COOPERATION

Michael Stürmer

The year 1990 was an annus mirabilis, but not the end of history—not in transatlantic relations, not in the contest with Russia and not in the European geometry of power. Still, things are not what they used to be: The organizing principle of the Cold War is lost; nuclear weapons no longer provide an organizing principle, and the economic currencies of power are ascendant. All of this, of course, deeply affects Franco-German security relations. The revolution of 1989 is only now fully unfolding. Change is everywhere, but what are the determining factors, the driving interests, the wider objectives? "Reculer pour mieux sauter," is not bad advice for today's analyst: so that the legacy of forty years of a stable bipolar and nuclear system is not lost for the present and for the future.

Except for the inescapable dictate of geography, Germany and France are an unlikely couple for military partnership, or even a broader security relationship. While the Germans, if left a choice, would opt for the marginal existence of Switzerland and Sweden, the French see themselves and their birthright in terms of "la grande nation." While the French accept that they were born to greatness, the Germans suffer when, as in 1990, greatness is thrust upon them. While the French see the ultimate truth in the nation state, the Germans fear the nation state and hope for redemption through European integration. While nationhood and the nation-state under central control has been the French form of political existence ever since the Sun King and the French Revolution, the Germans—if the demands of the welfare state, foreign affairs and economies of scale left them a choice—would consider themselves a collection of tribes with a common vernacular. Although reunification gave them a chance to reconsider, for most Germans the nation-state remains nothing but a remnant of the past. They prefer the "welfare state," with a particular emphasis on environmental virtue, and a "culture of restraint," qualities in which they are second to none.

Nevertheless, the Franco-German special relationship exists and the mystique goes back to the early postwar years. It should not be forgotten, of course, that in 1945 Charles de Gaulle wanted Germany carved up Richelieu style, and that it was U.S. President Harry S. Truman who had to convince the General that the new enemy was in the East. And in 1949, when the United States called NATO into existence and proposed a grand bargain—U.S. protection against Stalin's presence and Hitler's past if the Europeans would induct West Germany into their future economic community—it was French Foreign Minister Maurice Schuman who argued for Germany's neutral status. Two years later the French could accept, indeed promote the European Coal and Steel Community, but, in the end, could not accept the European Defense Community.

The same pattern has prevailed ever since. In economic affairs the two countries have worked together reasonably well, once the EEC was tailored to accommodate French agricultural products as well as German capital goods. For four decades, when it came to running the European Community, the European Monetary System and, above all, key appointments, the Franco-German relationship delivered. All of this was in spite of de Gaulle's rejection of British entry, his empty chair policy concerning agricultural markets, his confederal model of European Union (far from German visions) and his security monologue (incomprehensible to most of his German interlocutors). The partnership was oiled through an abundance of ministerial meetings, summits, and symbolism, not to mention some eminently practical friendships.

In fact, the European Union's functioning, whose theory remains, so far, remote from reality, does require a core group of those able and willing to act to take things in hand. Since France and Germany find the European Union a convenient framework both to enhance and to disguise their national interests, this core group, on the whole, works reasonably well. Whether it will continue to work as smoothly once EMU creates a formal core group with "Outs" as well as "Ins" is the key political question of the European Union's future, and will have to be dealt with before the queue of applicants from Eastern and Southern Europe can be admitted.

Security cooperation tells another story. Security policy is an expression of the sum total of a country's history, geography and vision of itself and the surrounding world. In the words of a celebrated French chanson, one could say that the French and German ideas of security are "deux rêves dans un seul lit." Each of the two dreams is saturated with the same history, but with a different version of it. One could say, of course, that both countries share the conviction that history must never repeat itself. But, beyond that, their paths diverge.

For most of French history, England had been the arch rival, whether it was the "Hundred Years War," the war of Spanish succession, the wars in North America and India, or the Napoleonic wars. Only after 1870, when Napoleon III declared war on Germany's first bid for national unity, did the French discover that the arch-enemy was living "outre Rhin." Until then, Germany was the chessboard and, on occasion, the battlefield for the projection of French power. Richelieu advised his king that he should rather part with a fat province than give up the "German Liberties," i.e., the right of German princes to side with France against the Emperor.

The generation of Charles de Gaulle grew up with a deeply ambiguous picture of Germany. That picture of a dynamic neighbor to be respected and feared dominated French strategic thinking from the organization of the school system after 1871 to the Dreyfus affair, from the agreements with Russia in 1891 to the reactions after Sarajevo in 1914—itself a tragedy far removed from either French or German vital interests but which nevertheless was transformed into the opening shots of the First World War. The war itself hardly softened French views of Germany. Jacques Bainville, the most popular historian of the post–World War I generation, criticized the Versailles Treaty as half-hearted and far too mild.

Thereafter the French felt betrayed both by the Americans, who left the continent, and by the British, who were willing to co-opt Germany. The result was the Ligne Maginot, more an expression of French fears than an effective defense against the Teutonic fury. While a distracted Third Republic moved to the verge of civil war, Nazi Germany developed its war machine. Trauma and mythology amplified the catastrophe that followed. The French saw the British leave them at Dunkerque to the bitterness of defeat and the humiliation of collaboration. The attacks on the French fleet at Oran and Mers el Kebir rubbed salt into French wounds and were never forgotten. In 1944 de Gaulle ordered his soldiers out of the allied column and diverted them to conquer Paris, although they wore U.S. uniforms and drove U.S. tanks. For de Gaulle, the Wehrmacht was more a transitory antagonist than the French communists who were more an eternal enemy. In the fall of the same year, de Gaulle took his revenge on those who had failed to invite him to Teheran and forged "la bonne et belle alliance" with Stalin, who looked to become the future master of Europe with the war over and the Anglo-Saxons again on the boats.

At Yalta, once again, there was no invitation to France, neither from Stalin nor from other quarters. De Gaulle prepared for the role of Europe's postwar chevalier seul. He was preoccupied with Germany and the ghosts of the nineteenth century; he did not anticipate Soviet expansionism and the realities of the Cold War, which would force France out of her Empire *outre mer* and into the dreaded role of an American dependency, unable to control her own national destiny. With the Soviet threat from without and the communist threat from within, France had no choice but to become part of the *Pax Americana*, which required treating Germany as an ally rather than an enemy.

During the decade that followed World War II and defined subsequent relations, France was torn between the goal of a European hegemony to contain Germany, finally resolved by the U.S. through NATO and by Great Britain through the WEU, and the goal of global containment of the Soviet Union, which had a presence on French soil via the communist party. The French learned painfully that NATO was of no help beyond the shores of Europe, as spelled out in Article VI of the Treaty. More precisely, NATO did not extend to Vietnam, Algeria, or Suez. Above all, as the U.S. nuclear monopoly gave way to strategic parity with the Soviet Union, France's old fears revived— being abandoned and left to burn in an isolated European theater or made the victim of conflicts in faraway parts of the world, like the Taiwan straits or Lebanon.

It was at this historical juncture, as the Fourth Republic cracked, that de Gaulle once again was called upon to be France's savior. The price was a final Adieu to the bloody stardust of the empire, which created, in turn, a fresh need to restore French morale: "Il faut faire le travail d'un psychiatre," de Gaulle told his Cabinet. Above all, he said, "il faut s'asseoir à la table des Grands."

The instrument chosen to pursue this policy was control over nuclear weapons—in the beginning not necessarily French ones, as de Gaulle was willing to accept U.S. weapons in French hands. This, however, conflicted sharply with U.S. instincts and interests and became unacceptable for U.S. policy after the nightmarish experiences of the Berlin and Cuba crises, in 1958 and 1962 respectively. Out of those crises, détente was born—the twin child of fear and reason. Thereafter, arms control with the Russians became the American priority. Once more, France was left out of decisions that would affect its own security. Great Britain was already privileged through its earlier special relationship with the U.S. Meanwhile, Europeans were offered an ill-defined and soon-aborted MLF. De Gaulle saw France not only being excluded from the table of "les Grands" but also, despite its status as one of the Four Powers sharing responsibility for Germany, being reduced in nuclear matters to the same modest level as the Federal Republic of Germany itself. So he canceled all plans for joint European programs—"le nucleaire se partage mal"—and proceeded with developing France's independent nuclear deterrent: "Tout s'organise en function de la force atomique." Through France's own force de dissuasion, de Gaulle could ensure that Germany remained a third-rate power, that the U.S. would never again be able to abandon France, that arms control could not proceed at the cost of French security, and that the Soviets gained a healthy respect for France's national interests. At one stroke and by her own national policy, France under de Gaulle banned the ghosts of the past and mastered the dangers of the present.

Germany's course offered a very different picture. While France was striving for independence, Germany under Chancellor Adenauer and all of his successors invariably translated every gain in national sovereignty into multilateralism. In the long run, Germany expected to gain more leverage through international institutions, above all NATO and the European Union, than through any isolated national role. Germany saw its past, including its nation-state, as a nightmare to be put in the archives of history. Atlanticism and Europe became the beacons of a better future, including the EEC's "ever closer union" that everybody, before Maastricht, was wise enough to leave undefined.

Admission to the European club came as early as 1952 through the European Coal and Steel Community—the merger of Germany's traditional weapons' forge on the Ruhr with her neighbors' own potential. Adenauer's renunciation of ABC weapons in 1954 paved the way toward WEU and NATO membership. In 1990, incidentally, that renunciation was confirmed, as a matter of course in the "Two-plus-Four-negotiations" without any major comment, let alone a Bundestag debate. Postwar Germans quickly understood that they could not assure their own security by their own national means. When they looked at the map of Central Europe they saw the exposed position of Berlin, their divided country and the Fulda Gap, and they thanked God for the U.S. presence. For Germany, NATO was both the wall of protection and the mark of being in the right club.

Of course, Adenauer, Franz-Josef Strauss, Helmut Schmidt, and Helmut Kohl all have realized that nuclear arms are weapons of a very special nature. Strauss, while keeping aloof from aspiring to any purely national deterrent, aimed for a collective European deterrent together with France and Italy. His strategic reasons were precisely the same as those that prompted de Gaulle to aim for French nuclear weapons after 1958. But the trilateral agreement of 1958 to build a French-

German-Italian deterrent was not to flourish. It was canceled by de
Gaulle. Shortly thereafter, the American multilateral version, the MLF,
was sunk by the Kennedy administration before it ever set sail. The
German government, while signing the Non-Proliferation Treaty, con-
tented itself with a seat at NATO's Nuclear Planning Group. Thus,
the Germans, while not in physical control of nuclear weapons, got
a seat "à la table des Grands." Meanwhile, the F-104 Starfighter, the
203 mm howitzers and the short-range missiles provided Germany
with nuclear platforms, even if she still had no nuclear weapons of
her own. In an era increasingly driven by the demands of arms control,
however, these platforms were more than a consolation prize. The
NATO solution to Germany's aspirations had the additional charm
that the nuclear weapons debate in Germany would be largely forgotten
for at least a decade. Instead, the Germans engaged in *Neue Ostpolitik,*
the détente variety encouraged, indeed demanded by Germany's Western allies, who nevertheless looked upon it with no small amount
of suspicion.

This era of deterrence, détente and German *Ostpolitik,* embodied
in NATO's Harmel report and MC14-3, put heavy strains on the
Franco-German security relationship, notwithstanding the Elysée
Treaty of 1963 and a never ending string of consultations. The Germans, whose attention was riveted twenty-four hours a day to the
enormous Soviet forces on the central front, saw the French keep their
forces almost exclusively west of Baden-Baden and, in any event,
neglecting their conventional forces. While NATO adopted flexible
response and a counterforce nuclear strategy, the French, for political as
well as technical reasons, stuck to massive retaliation—never answering
German questions about the expected use of French "prestrategic"
nuclear weapons or where exactly the notorious "dernier avertissement"
was targeted.

Unexpectedly, France was brought closer to NATO and her
German ally through the renewed Soviet threat embodied in the INF
deployments that started in 1975 and were countered by NATO's
double track decision four years later. President Mitterrand used the
occasion of the twentieth anniversary of the Elysée Treaty to deliver

his celebrated "discours au Bundestag" in January 1983. He not only supported the Kohl-Genscher government's stand on the deployment of U.S. Pershings and cruise missiles but also made clear that policy makers in Paris were painfully aware of the "destin commun" between France and Germany. In 1985, French troops in large numbers were seen at the Danube in the bilateral exercises called "Moineau Hardi." Soon the Franco-German brigade was called into being, straddling both sides of the Rhine while leaving the more delicate questions of command and control undecided.

The 1980s registered a gradual rapprochement of France with WEU, especially after 1987. In French eyes German Foreign Minister Hans-Dietrich Genscher put too much faith in the CSCE. In effect, whenever French policymakers thought they could take the Germans for granted, they cultivated French strategic independence. But whenever the Germans showed signs of thinking "à la française," the French became more NATO-minded. Genscher's speech in Davos on February 1, 1987, urging that Gorbachev be taken at his word prompted *Le Monde* to speak of "Le gorbasme allemand," and reminded the French both of NATO's charms and the role of the Four Powers who had borne, since 1945, responsibility for "Germany as a whole."

The famous night in November 1989 that ended the Cold War after four decades also ended the comforts of France's ambivalence toward NATO. The old balance of imbalances could no longer be maintained. The "Two-plus-Four" train toward German unification, with Gorbachev, Bush, Baker, and Kohl on the locomotive, could not be stopped. Any thought of a French game *à trois* with Britain and Russia to keep the two Germanies divided, if it ever crossed Mitterrand's mind after the German Chancellor's ten-point speech on November 28, 1989, was merely a conditioned reflex from old French nightmares, not something for daylight. So France had to show satisfaction at getting rid of her share of four-power control and be consoled with the news that the whole of Germany would be in NATO with German troops capped at 370,000 and the old renunciation of ABC weapons reiterated.

At the Gulf in 1991, while united Germany was unwilling to impress the world with a military contribution (not even a hospital ship anchored off the coast of Saudi Arabia), France was present with a light tank dirigion, once again an effort *à tenir le rang,* more precisely to show both alliance solidarity and global aspirations. But the actual significance of this particular action for French policy was less distinct than its symbolic character. After "Two-plus Four" had closed the books on World War II, the European Union became the arena for a new attempt to define Franco-German relations. The European Union—so far an economic framework in search of political purpose—now had to develop a foreign policy role, or remain forever a free trade zone deluxe. At the same time, the European Union had also to define its own structure more than in the past, in order to determine the role of both Germany and France.

This was the real agenda driving the IGCs of the 1990s on EMU and Political Union. EMU, springing from the accumulated political-economic *acquis communautaire* of the past thirty-five years, is an elaborately planned project of manifest significance. Political Union rests on some formal compromises designed to satisfy the distinctly anti-integrationist views of the British; the French are happy not to have to lead any of the battles for it. In fact, they are themselves in both the camp of economic integration and the camp of continuing political and security independence. As a result, the EMU dossier is replete with criteria and calendar, and it promises the French release from the "monstre de Francfort." By contrast, the Political Union dossier, in spite of all the German vows, is vague to the point of caricature concerning the CFSP and the role of the WEU. Not even appearances were saved.

As there is no attempt at defining the European security interest over and above any national interest, the security dimension of Maastricht is difficult to describe in terms that would impress any potential enemy. To describe the WEU as the "bras armé" of the European Union, or the European pillar of NATO, would be far ahead of reality. In theory, the CFSP could provide the glue for both common analyses and joint action. But in practice it is to be divided between four

Commissioners, with the President of the Commission unwilling to be the foreign policy Czar, hardly a bureaucratic structure to support it, and scarcely a diplomatic service beyond economic affairs to represent it. So the Council of Ministers will tend to foreign affairs with little willingness to take substance away from nation-states. The European Union will thus continue to be strong in commercial diplomacy and sadly non-existent for any meaningful dimension beyond. Thus, while the European Union is currently headed toward EMU, including a powerful steering committee of the participants, in the security field the European Union will, prudence being the better part of valor, continue to be "la grande muette." A European superstate is not on the agenda. Not even a major player in the foreign policy field is likely to emerge out of the European Union's rendezvous with reality.

So there must be other channels for the Franco-German security relationship: The Eurocorps, OSCE, WEU, and, inevitably, NATO. But the Eurocorps—organized around the Franco-German brigade with a German heavy tank division and a light French one, headquarters at Strasbourg, and Belgian and Spanish contingents—represents more the disunity than the unity of purpose between France and Germany. The differences have grown rather than diminished, not only in technical terms but even more in philosophical terms. This has put the future of the Eurocorps in question. The French can see it as a potential fighting force in "out of area" contingencies, while the Germans still regard it as a bridge between NATO and France and not, in the words of the German Defense Minister, "an Afrikakorps." France's surprise transition to "l'armee du metier" and Germany's continuing belief in conscription will exacerbate the differences further. While France braces herself to build an intervention force of global and certainly Middle East/North Africa reach, the Germans (government, opposition, and general public) find it difficult to raise their sights beyond Article V of the Washington Treaty and the Petersberg 1993 catalogue, i.e. peacekeeping but not peace enforcement.

Recently, however, Bosnia furnished some lessons about post–Cold War realities. Given the demise of the Red Army, today's threats come from far afield and are often not predominantly military, or even well-organized. Their catalogue includes nuclear proliferation, demographic revolution, political collapse, rogue states, state supported terrorism, and organized crime. Such threats are often directed not against national borders, but against the fabric of society. This fundamental shift has not yet found adequate expression in political and strategic thinking, although France is perhaps further along than Germany.

Philosophically and politically the two countries, although living within the same strategic space, see themselves in different worlds and react through different and not necessarily complementary strategies. Germany tries not to think in terms of deterrence, nuclear or conventional. Instead, it pursues its security through building a secure neighborhood to its East and South. It knits its few remaining divisions into multinational corps, an approach more geared to reassuring friends than fighting enemies, and highly dependent on a continuing U.S. presence. France takes a more proactive approach, although one that is based on an overstretched economy.

While the Germans are optimistic and believe in architecture, the French are pessimistic and believe in deterrence and, if necessary, intervention. Both countries, however, understand that the time for national defense will not come back and that their armaments industries require both more synergy and quality as envisaged but not realized in the Maastricht Treaty. Here again, history and geography make themselves felt, despite the prospects for economies of scale and the professions of elective affinities. The Germans are reluctant sellers of arms, principally only to friends in peaceful regions, while the French prefer a more robust approach. Cooperating with the Germans is, therefore, often seen as a lesser option.

Both countries, much as in the past, build their security on NATO. The Germans see this as a virtue, the French as a necessity. NATO, in this context, means above all the U.S. presence, which is needed for the following purposes:

> To reassure Europeans in general, and East Europeans in particular, against the residual Soviet threat;

- To protect Europe against the global risks of the future;
- To restrain the clashing national claims that remain in Europe, including those of Greece and Turkey; and
- To continue holding the old demons of European history at bay.

This American role can only continue in the context of a new transatlantic bargain. It cannot be dictated from outside. It must be the product of foresight, strategic thinking and leadership on both sides of the Atlantic. There would be advantages for the United States.

It could secure a controlling stake in Europe at a modest price, and act as a kind of holding company for Europe. Such an American role would restrain the emergence of new nuclear players, whether among or with the help of Europeans. And provided the Americans were prepared to share setting their world agenda, it would secure a truly global role for the United States rather than the mere status that goes along with being the world's greatest, most secure island.

For the Europeans, however, this continuing American role comes at a price. The need to merge their security roles and responsibilities effectively will not have to become an overriding common goal. They can continue the game of "everybody for himself and the United States for us all." Thus, in spite of the double arch of crisis surrounding Europe and all the uncertainties of the wider world, an overriding European strategic interest will be unlikely to emerge soon. The European Union, despite the high flying formulas of the Maastricht Treaty, will for some time continue to be an economic giant with a lot of commercial clout, but a political dwarf with a hollow CFSP. Machiavelli, if he had to advise the U.S. President, might whisper into his ear that this state of affairs is not unattractive and simplifies matters for Washington.

For the Europeans, it will merely continue a familiar dilemma. The nation state of European dimension—whether France, Italy, Britain or Germany—can only be a third rate player in the world. But Europe's nation-states continue to love their little differences more than their common destiny. What acts as their source of strength in cultural terms is their source of weakness in international security. The EU's imbalance between economic strength and political weakness will continue, and no amount of Euro-rhetoric will end it. As long as the United States is around to protect the Europeans against the consequences of their disunity, neither the existential need nor the vital energy to forge a power on the European side of the Atlantic will arise. The rendezvous with reality cannot, of course, wait forever. The Franco-German security relationship is part and parcel of this state of affairs. For the time being, it requires an act of faith to see it as the organizing principle of a major world player called Europe.

EMU AND THE FRANCO-GERMAN RELATIONSHIP

Jean-Pierre Landau

From the point of view of the Franco-German economic relationship, there are two ways of looking at EMU. One could say that the prospect of EMU has triggered a very powerful dynamic of integration, which goes far beyond the creation of a single currency and monetary union. EMU embodies fiscal as well as monetary policies. It will create in Europe a financial market and currency zone that will change the nature and working of the international monetary system. It will lead to further and deeper economic and financial integration. It might, even should, culminate with some form of political union. This is what could be called the optimistic view.

The pessimistic view would be as follows: if implemented, EMU will be a source of tension between participating countries to a point that will exacerbate rather than eliminate Europe's division. This is because the politics of EMU are unrealistic and, above all, the economics are wrong. The attempt to impose a unified monetary policy on countries that have not reached the same degree of labor market flexibility, let alone the same aversion to inflation, will inevitably increase unemployment and create frustration and resentment. This view is most commonly held in some circles of non-continental Europe and the United States. The same circles often doubt the appropriateness of present European monetary policies.

I myself strongly hold the optimistic view of EMU. But I also recognize that success cannot be taken for granted. Ultimately, it will rest on our common ability—especially French and German—

to deepen and broaden our mutual understanding of how economic and monetary policy should be conducted in Europe. No institutional mechanisms or safeguards, however necessary, can compensate for the lack of a shared vision of our economic future. In short, we have to converge in our minds as extensively as we converge in our acts and economic performances. Only with the full support of our respective publics will it be possible to undertake the changes necessary in our economies. This is our agenda for the period ahead.

The Rationale for EMU

There is no denying the political attractions of EMU. The project fits well into the historical tradition of European integration. It creates a new "common policy" through which member states can jointly pursue mutually beneficial objectives and, thereby, strengthen their solidarity and unity. It associates, in a first stage, a core of countries that later may be joined by others. This is exactly how European integration has progressed since the early 1950s.

But EMU should not be judged merely on its political merits, even if most American experts think that we have engaged ourselves, for political reasons, in a hopeless monetary venture that will bring severe hardship to our economies and people.

In fact, there is a very strong economic rationale for EMU. The theoretical analysis of the costs and benefits of monetary integration was spelled out thirty years ago, as were the conditions for its success. One could be forgiven for not being totally convinced that European integration fits those conditions. Europe is definitely not an "optimum currency area," at least not yet. Differences in language and culture will for a long time constitute an irreducible obstacle to the very labor mobility that, according to the theory, is a precondition for the smooth functioning of a monetary union. Wage flexibility in European countries is not sufficient to compensate for immobility. Nevertheless, three considerations, taken together, fully justify the move to EMU.

First, the Single Market cannot work in the long run, unless European countries achieve a high degree of real and nominal exchange rate stability. I am aware that this is a very controversial proposition. Numerous studies have failed to identify any significant impact of exchange rate variability on international trade and investment. But there is no historical precedent for the level of economic integration that has been achieved among the separate countries of the European Union. To some extent, their economies are now more integrated than those of the individual states in the U.S. Thus, real exchange-rate movements can be expected to have a bigger impact than what is commonly assumed among national economies elsewhere, and we cannot simply transpose the empirical results of existing studies that were conducted in a different environment.

In any case, the Single Market is more than just a free trade area. It is about creating an economic space where relative competitive positions are not influenced by government policies, whether of a micro- or macroeconomic nature. To further that objective, governments in the EU have achieved very strict disciplines on microeconomic interventions, whether financial or regulatory, which would distort competition. This is expected to generate significant gains in efficiency and resource allocation. But these could easily be wiped out if relative prices are subject to unpredictable shifts of real exchange rates or market sentiment.

Second, exchange-rate stability cannot be sustained in Europe without monetary union. In theory, it should be possible to achieve a sufficient degree of exchange-rate stability without going all the way to a full-fledged monetary union. Indeed, that was the original purpose of the European Monetary System (EMS), which worked reasonably well until European countries moved to generalize freedom of capital movements. Since then, it has been more difficult to manage the system, as events in 1992–93 have amply demonstrated. To preserve the EMS at all, broad margins have been needed which allow very significant movements in both nominal and real exchange rates. In theory, again, such fluctuations are unnecessary if monetary policies and inflation rates converge. But I cannot help drawing one clear conclusion from the events of July 1993: convergence is a necessary condition for exchange rate stability, but ultimately not a sufficient one.

If we accept that it might be difficult in the future to operate a system of narrow bands with full capital mobility on a permanent basis, then we are faced with a simple alternative: either we accept the prospect of potential exchange rate instability between European countries, which, in the end, might put unsustainable strains on the Single Market; or we move to monetary union. EMU thus appears as the natural, indeed indispensable complement to the Single Market.

Finally, one of the main benefits of EMU is going to occur through the creation of a large financial market in instruments denominated in euros. That market will eventually equal the dollar market in size, liquidity, and depth. In the long run, this might bring significant changes to international monetary and financial relations. Very quickly, those financial institutions that operate in the euro will be offered numerous new business opportunities and gain competitive advantage. From a macroeconomic point of view, European growth should benefit from lower interest rates as exchange rate risk disappears and, very likely, as significant capital inflows follow. European financial institutions seem more and more aware of such opportunities and, accordingly, are committing significant resources to prepare for EMU, which, in itself increases the probability that EMU will eventually happen. Correspondingly, there is apprehension in those countries that initially may decide not to participate. There is little doubt that the dynamics of a unified financial market will work strongly in favor of further economic integration; countries that stay out may see themselves, *de facto*, excluded.

Franco-German Convergence

EMU is not a purely a Franco-German endeavor. But it would not have been possible without a strong commitment from both countries and increased convergence between our economies. Fluctuations in market sentiment about EMU closely follow assessments of the quality of the Franco-German relationship. Convergence has gone a long way in the last few years. There is now no difference between French and German performances in inflation. In fact, during the years following German reunification, French inflation has been consistently lower. Accordingly, differentials in long-term interest rates have all but disappeared in normal times, even if, admittedly, they rise again in periods of exchange-rate tension. Cyclical fluctuations are increasingly parallel and long-run growth performance is nearly identical (with slightly faster growth in France).

While nominal convergence has been achieved, some argue that "real" divergences are still there. In particular, they point to France's higher unemployment rate and, more recently, to a better German performance in bringing the fiscal deficit under control. Since those facts do influence public perception about the benefits of EMU and the probability that it will take place (according to the Maastricht requirements), they deserve some comment.

In the fiscal sphere, the German achievement has, by all means, been remarkable. I would explain the relative deterioration of the French position by the peculiarities of the political cycle, with no less than three national elections between 1993 and 1998 (one presidential and two parliamentary). Nevertheless, we are now back on track to meet the Maastricht criteria. For the first time since 1945, the recently adopted budget for 1997 provides for a reduction in overall expenditures so that, unless economic growth is unexpectedly weak in 1997, the deficit target of three percent of GDP will be met.

Unemployment is the biggest French problem today. The relationship between unemployment and EMU is complex. I would note, in this regard, that economic growth in France since 1987 has been higher, on average, than in European countries which have opted for a different monetary policy (although this might not be true for the last three years). Thus, the main causes for unemployment are found in the rigidities of the labor market (while differences with Germany can partly be attributed to divergent demographic trends). As for unemployment and Franco-German convergence from the perspective of monetary union, what should probably be considered is not the respective absolute levels of unemployment, which, unfortunately, are both high, but the relative flexibility of wages in response to a shock.

In this latter respect, there doesn't seem to be any significant difference between the two countries.

This being said, continued high unemployment in France may fuel the perception of the public and financial markets that present monetary and exchange-rate policies are politically unsustainable and that, at some stage, they will be reversed. While clearly wrong, this perception creates additional uncertainty and may result in higher interest rates and permanent instability on the foreign exchange market. This, in my view, is a strong reason not to delay the beginning of Phase III of EMU beyond the normal date of January 1, 1999.

Managing the Euro

Much remains to be done to ensure that the European Central Bank (ECB) will enjoy both the same credibility and public support as our two national central banks do today. This cannot be taken for granted. On the German side, there are signs of public doubt that the euro will be as sound and non-inflationary a currency as the DM has been. We can, therefore, expect the ECB to be especially vigilant in establishing its credibility in its first few years of operation. It is likely, therefore, to err on the side of caution when in doubt about the appropriate stance of monetary policy.

On the French side, it is obvious for anyone reading the daily newspaper that not everybody agrees with the idea of a monetary policy oriented toward the goal of price stability. The public debate on monetary policy in France is an opportunity for some leaders to express frustration at the loss of what they see as an important economic policy tool. But it should be remembered that doubts about the current policy, although given wide voice, come from a limited circle of academic, political and business elites. Quite often, they are echoed by statements from prestigious U.S. academics, which even tend to give them an aura of credibility.

In theory, the Treaty provides for a clear allocation of responsibilities: the independent ECB conducts the EMU's monetary policy while the Council, made up of Ministers of Finance, defines the EMU's exchange-rate policy. In practice, these are closely related matters and it is difficult to consider the exchange rate as an independent variable, once monetary policy has been decided. Furthermore, even an independent central bank keeps an eye on the exchange rate, whether it is considered an indicator of monetary conditions or an implicit or explicit target.

The question will soon be solved insofar as it concerns the relationship between the euro and the currencies of the non-EMU members of the European Union (the so called "ins" and "outs" issue). It has now been made clear that any future arrangement for fixed but adjustable rates will not require the ECB to support weak currencies and thus will fully preserve the ability of the ECB to conduct its monetary policy independently. Membership of this very asymmetric system will be voluntary, however. The possibility will remain open for free-riding Single-Market participants to improve their competitive positions by devaluing their currencies. I personally believe this will not be a major problem. EU countries not participating in the EMU at the outset will very quickly want to converge in order to join.

A different situation might arise over the euro's exchange rate and those of non-European currencies. ECB monetary policy will be strict and portfolio diversification by non-European investors will induce capital inflows into the euro financial market. At present, member countries of the EMS still have the option of asking for a realignment if they feel that the evolution of exchange rates outside Europe has damaged their overall competitiveness. With EMU that possibility will vanish. As a result, external exchange-rate movements might bring durable shocks to specific areas (or countries) of EMU. There is a "real" aspect to such a situation which might lend legitimacy to government demands on the exchange rate as provided in the Treaty. On the other hand, the ECB will rightly resist any attempt to change the course of monetary policy purely on the basis of exchange rate considerations (unless, of course, governments participating in EMU have entered an international agreement committing them to exchange rate targets). No clear recipe exists for dealing with such a situation. Increased flexibility in labor markets would certainly help.

So, I suspect, would the possibility of using fiscal policy to compensate partially shocks that were asymmetric within the E.U.

Through the "excessive deficit" procedure, fiscal policies of EMU members will be subjected to strict discipline. There are, of course, very good reasons for doing so. Every country is subject to the same fiscal criteria, e.g. accumulated debt to GDP ratio or annual deficit to GDP ratio, etc. It might have been considered whether the determination of what is an excessive deficit at any given time should be judged in terms of a structural, rather than current balance, so as to eliminate the impact of business-cycle fluctuations.

The stability pact, whose principle has been adopted in 1996, will remedy some of these problems. It is to be hoped that it will help and improve, at the same time, the quality of economic policy decision making inside the EMU. Even if we do not assume that fiscal policy has any impact on output in the long run, it can still help smooth fluctuations in the short term. Also, governments should keep open the possibilities for absorbing asymmetric shocks through coordinated moves in their national budgets. In the U.S., it is estimated that about 35 percent of any shock occurring in a specific state is automatically compensated through the federal budget. There is no comparable federal budget in Europe. Hence the necessity for stronger coordination among national budgets.

Please allow me one last word about structural reform, although it is outside the realm of this paper. Structural reform is obviously an urgent necessity, both to ensure the increased flexibility needed for the EMU to function smoothly, and in general to adjust our economies to the changing world environment. France and Germany face the same challenge, and in similar terms. As is normal, there is a healthy competition between countries over the speed and efficiency of their adjustment process. But it is also an area for deeper cooperation. If they want to ensure joint prosperity for the coming decades, governments should find it appropriate to stress to their electorates the commonality of challenges and purposes that our two countries share.

FRANCO-GERMAN ECONOMIC RELATIONS

Ernst Welteke

Probably no other bilateral relationship influences economic and political life in Europe as much as Franco-German cooperation. It is the true catalyst for European integration. The start of the European Monetary Union on January 1, 1999—unimaginable without the two countries—will be a historical beat of the drum for the end of this century.

In recent decades, decision makers in Bonn and Paris have realized that economic cooperation between their countries was inevitable and that its success was of foremost importance for Europe. Starting with the Treaty of Rome in 1957, and continuing with the establishment of the European Monetary System and the Single Market, Franco-German initiatives have led to the Maastricht Treaty, which has laid down the foundations for the European Union. Today, this unique relationship is even more important because of the globalization of markets.

It would be useful to share some figures on the combined economic significance of the two countries in a global as well as European context: France and Germany represent fifteen percent of total world GNP. Their share of world trade is even higher, at seventeen percent. Both countries together account for some fourteen percent of all foreign direct investment worldwide. With forty percent of the population of the European Union, the two countries produce fifty percent of total EU output.

This dominance is also true in financial and monetary terms. Seventeen percent of all international bonds are issued in either German marks or French francs. Together, both countries make up more than fifty percent of the basket value of the European Currency Unit (ECU).

In spite of their importance in the world economy, doubts have recently arisen in Germany and France over their competitiveness compared to other industrialized nations and fast-growing emerging economies. At the root of such doubts are certain structural difficulties almost identical in both countries. The most prominent ones were the subject of a recent *World Economic Outlook* of the IMF. It focused on high public indebtedness, runaway social security and health care costs, and inflexible labor market conditions. Calls for corrective measures are widely heard. According to the IMF, progress in budgetary consolidation is evident but still insufficient.

Fiscal problems receive further attention because of the importance placed on fiscal soundness as a criterion for accession to the European Monetary Union. France and Germany, like almost all other EU countries, are endeavoring not to run up "excessive deficits." While the inflation, interest and exchange rate criteria—spelled out in the Maastricht Treaty—are widely fulfilled, the requirement of "no excessive deficit" still causes problems.

President Chirac and Chancellor Kohl have recently underscored their commitment to cut deficits and adhere strictly to the stipulations of the Treaty. The budget drafts for 1997, presented by German and French Finance Ministers Theo Waigel and Jean Arthuis, envisage budget deficits of three percent or even lower.

General economic developments will play a crucial role. The latest figures point to a moderately accelerating business cycle. In the first half of this year, German and French GNP grew by identical rates, which is true also for the average of the last five years. The IMF has projected similar growth rates for both at 1.3 percent in 1996 and 2.4 percent in 1997, respectively. These figures are at the upper end of the forecast spectrum. This would mean an encouraging macroeconomic development and support fiscal consolidation.

Like almost all European states, both countries suffer the same malady of stubbornly high unemployment. In Germany, for example, the rate is approximately ten percent, in France twelve. It is widely believed that an economic upswing alone will not improve the situation noticeably, as joblessness is increasingly viewed as structural in nature.

Of course, competition between French and German companies on world markets is keen, sometimes with national prestige at stake. Take, for example, the worldwide competition between French and German firms to sell their high-speed trains. The relationship between the financial centers of Paris and Frankfurt is also defined by competition rather than cooperation, with each aspiring to become the number one financial center on the European continent.

Apart from competing with each other on world markets, our two countries are connected by a complex network of joint ventures, e.g. the Franco-German industrial project, Airbus Industries. The mutual flow of capital investment is intensifying. France is a favorite location for German foreign direct investment, eighteen percent of which went to France in 1995. The reverse is also true. In 1995 about eight percent of FDI in Germany came from France.

Franco-German trade represents the most important bilateral trade relationship in the European Union, in addition to being one of the greatest in the world. Not surprisingly, each is the other's principal trading partner. Our foreign trade with France amounts to about eleven percent of aggregate German foreign trade. The corresponding share of French trade with Germany adds up to seventeen percent of the aggregate. Last year Germany exported goods and services totalling sixty billion marks to France while spending fifty billion marks on French imports. Traditionally, bilateral trade has shown a surplus in favor of Germany. Nevertheless, it is my impression that, at least in everyday life, French products in Germany are more common than vice versa. French wine and cheese are part of our lifestyle, and owning certain French automobiles signifies individualism.

The impression of synchronism is also emphasized by price figures. On both sides of the Rhine, inflation is currently of no concern, with annual rates near 1.5 percent. At the same time, interest rates on mark and franc fixed-income bonds are very similar for short and long-term maturities.

From a mere monetary point of view, a rosier scenario for European Monetary Union is hard to imagine. For years, French monetary and economic policies have pursued a course oriented toward preserving price stability. This was reinforced by granting independence to the Banque de France in 1993. Given this background, no one should be too concerned if now and then French politicians demand a more expansive monetary policy for addressing the urgent economic problems. This sometimes occurs in Germany as well. What is more important is that the central banks do not yield to these temptations. Even before the governors of the respective central banks met regularly, a consensus existed to reject such simplistic solutions. As this consensus is real, no real concern is warranted about what will happen to stability when the European Central Bank assumes monetary sovereignty.

Despite the strong degree of convergence, however, short-term exchange rate fluctuations do still surface to interfere with the smooth functioning of the Single Market. Even in a relatively quiet year like this, variations in the mark/franc exchange rate of more than two percent have occurred. The European Monetary Union will eliminate exchange rate fluctuations as a factor of interference, thus putting economic relations in Europe on a more solid footing.

In addition, today's European Monetary Union is imperative as ever given the challenges of globalization and continuing dollar fluctuations, whose causes may or may not be economically based. In the past, French and German firms have suffered repeatedly from shocks due to abrupt changes of the external value of the dollar. A united Europe, as an economic and financial counterweight to the United States, could better absorb such shocks by reducing its dependence on foreign markets. On average, the ratio of exports subject to fluctuating exchange rates for all EU countries currently stands at 28 percent, for imports 26 percent. In a united Europe of fifteen states, these figures would fall to 11 percent, a level of trade dependency of U.S. proportions.

Of course, the EMU will have advantages much closer to home. Allow me to point out the obvious. Exchange and hedging costs in Europe, costs estimated to be forty billion marks per year, will disappear at once. At the very least, this will mean easier access for small and medium-sized firms to European markets. Banks, to be sure, will lose a certain share of their foreign exchange trading. Paris will be more affected than Frankfurt, because the trading of EU currencies dominates the French market, whereas Frankfurt is stronger in dollar trading. But, compared to the positive effects of monetary union for the whole economy, such losses will be negligible. The following will count far more:

• Trade in goods and services in Europe will become increasingly transparent and free of exchange rate uncertainties, thereby stimulating competition and growth.

• Calculations for long-term investments at home or in other European countries will be based on a more secure foundation and, therefore, made easier.

• The increased capitalization of the European financial markets will translate into more capital available for companies and a tendency towards lower interest rates.

Monetary Union is not, per se, a job creation package. But, insofar as EMU strengthens competition and fuels economic growth, it should also yield positive results for employment over the long run. Yet, arriving at an acceptable level of employment under today's conditions requires more than strong growth.

In this regard (as the former President of the Bundesbank, Professor Schlesinger, recently noted), Monetary Union could also bring about a real structural transformation that goes beyond market competition to a "competition of systems." This means a competition between different mixtures of taxes, regulation, and social welfare.

Some of our rigid and inflexible structures could be cracked open, and the result should be more employment.

As it is, structural barriers still hinder the expansion of the job creating service sectors in our countries. The output of the service sectors in France, as well as in Germany, amounts to only about two-thirds of GNP compared to three-quarters of GNP in the U.S. All in all, monetary union promises to make European companies more competitive and better prepared for the new challenges of globalization.

Let me turn now to some of the EMU's political implications. Wage negotiations will have to take into consideration, more than ever, the different conditions in the various European countries, particularly the uneven levels of productivity. In other words, wages should be more closely tied to productivity. It would be unwise to ignore this principle by attempting to impose income parity throughout Europe. This would inevitably lead to greater joblessness as well as the inclination to step up state transfers within the EU. This risk has to be anticipated and countered in advance.

A single European currency will also eliminate the sanctions now imposed by foreign exchange markets on unsound national economic or fiscal policies. Since the success of the EMU requires, however, especially solid financial policies, Mr. Theo Waigel, Germany's Minister of Finance, has proposed an "internal stability pact" to ensure such policies. There is now general agreement on this and it represents very tangible political progress. The stability pact will oblige all states to keep their financial houses in order, not only at the time they enter into the monetary union, but over the long term, i.e. after they are inside. In Germany, now, as well as in other European states, major efforts are being undertaken to trim public deficits. These efforts would be necessary with or without the EMU in order to strengthen our competitiveness and, therefore, our long-run economic prosperity. The stability pact will help us to guard our present accomplishments in the future.

Undoubtedly, the European Central Bank that has been designed for the EMU—to be located in Frankfurt—is the outstanding feature of the entire project. With its commitment to price stability and its independence from political pressure, the ECB will ensure that the single currency, the euro, remains stable.

Finally, let me reflect on the relationship between EMU and EU enlargement. At present, ten east and central European countries have signed association agreements with the EU and applied for membership (Poland, Czech Republic, Slovakia, Hungary, Slovenia, Bulgaria, Romania, Estonia, Latvia, Lithuania). It is absolutely necessary that countries wishing to join the E.U. endorse the objective of monetary union and adjust their economic policies accordingly. The EMU is part of the European Union's *acquis communautaire*, i.e., part of the core body of EU legislation.

To qualify for monetary union, however, even countries like the Czech Republic and Hungary still need to introduce important economic changes. They have particular difficulty with the EMU's inflation and interest rate criteria. Central bank independence is another critical difficulty for them. Indeed, the banking systems in most aspiring countries are currently in some distress, the result mainly of the abrupt change from centrally planned to market oriented systems. With technical assistance from EU central banks, these countries are now trying to establish the necessary adjustment process in their financial and monetary sectors. But the adjustments are not easy. There is probably some truth in forecasts that see the first of the applicant countries qualifying for the EMU, at the earliest, about ten years from now.

Allow me to close by recalling the fundamental reality that spurs our efforts: The significance of the European Monetary Union transcends the economic sphere. It is the vehicle for deepening European integration. It will ensure peaceful coexistence in Europe, with the Franco-Goman relationship as the vanguard for Europe's future, as it has been throughout the postwar era.

THE FRANCO-GERMAN AXIS
FROM DE GAULLE TO CHIRAC

Patrick McCarthy

Gaullist Origins

It might be useful, before analyzing what the Franco-German axis is, to state briefly what it is not. It was never designed to dissolve two nation-states into some larger, unnamed entity. Even less was it meant to constitute the core of a supranational Europe. In speaking of Germany in 1945, de Gaulle states that it will not be a "Reich" but its "peuple" will survive Hitler. As for France it too has a peuple, but it is also to re-become an état.[1]

Secondly, the Franco-German relationship is not to take in Britain as an equal member. In 1945 de Gaulle sees the Britain of the Second World War as an essential, sometimes generous and sometimes perfidious ally. Looking ahead, he sees Britain as part of the Anglo-Saxon "camp." So Anglo-French relations are to become less close, although Britain is still a European country, and, hence the closest ally outside of the continental European countries. The United States, Britain's partner in the Anglo-Saxon "camp," belongs among the non-European nations. After reaching agreements, France and Germany, with or without other continental European partners, will negotiate first with Britain and then, once an agreement is reached, with the U.S.

This article was originally written for *Europa/Europe*, where it appeared in Italian in 1997. I wish to thank the editors of the magazine for permission to use the English version.

To state what the Franco-German relationship was, is more difficult. In 1944, when he made his visit to the Soviet Union, de Gaulle's
goals were to liberate France both from the old German threat and
from the new Anglo-Saxon hegemony. He takes what one might call
the Poincaré view of Germany: it is to be kept in subjection; it must
be too weak to harm France. Germany is to be divided: the left bank
of the Rhine, supposedly autonomous, will be dominated by France,
the Ruhr will be under international control and the Oder-Neisse will
form the Eastern border. A Franco-Soviet pact will guarantee that
Germany remains dismembered. It will also protect a Europe, that
now includes the USSR as an integral member, against the Anglo-
Saxon camp.[2]

So the USSR is France's privileged partner. Britain belongs already
to a special category: it is both a member of the Anglo-Saxon group
and European, although not fully European. The U.S. is outside
Europe, the leader of the Anglo-Saxon group and the world's strongest
nation tempted by the will to dominate. Agreements are reached in
the way already described, except that the USSR occupies what will
be Germany's place. But the trip to Moscow, brilliantly described in
de Gaulle's memoirs, does not bring the results he had sought. The
Franco-Soviet Treaty[3] states that the two countries will cooperate
closely after the war is won but it does not mention the division of
Germany along the lines set out by de Gaulle.

The reason goes beyond the dispute over Poland and beyond
generic notions of evil Communists. The USSR simply did not consider
France a strong enough power and wanted to deal directly with the
Anglo-Saxons. Yalta was Stalin's preferred forum. This is the first of
three occasions when France attempts to maintain control over Germany by establishing a privileged relationship with the USSR and
each attempt ends in failure. De Gaulle's opening to the East in the
1960s did not prevent the Soviets from giving priority to reaching an
agreement with Nixon in the early 1970s. More glaring was Mitterrand's failure, at his meeting with Gorbachev in the autumn 1989,
to create a Franco-Soviet alliance that would oversee German Reunification. Gorbachev preferred to deal directly with the Kohl government.

After the first and third of these failures, France decided to give priority to the relationship with Germany, even if the forms that the relationship took were very different. By the time that the first phase of the Franco-German relationship took shape in the European Coal and Steel Community (ECSC) of 1950, the Cold War had transformed the USSR into the dominant threat. This reduced the importance of the threats represented by Germany and by Anglo-Saxon hegemony. Indeed, it forced France into an alliance with Germany and it increased French dependence on the U.S. By now de Gaulle had left power, and his successors did not ascribe the same importance to foreign policy.[4] Yet the impact of de Gaulle's period of power remained and certain elements of his thought provided the underpinnings of French foreign policy.

The first was the importance of the state which must be interventionist at home in order to build the strong nation that could defend French interests abroad. In 1945 de Gaulle spells out the link between the nationalization of basic industries or the founding of L'Ecole nationale d'administration and the assertion of French rights within the wartime alliance. In 1954 de Gaulle helped torpedo the European Defense Community (EDC) because of its supranational structure.

Nor was de Gaulle's distrust of the U.S. banished by the Cold War. As he explained to Roosevelt's envoy, Harry Hopkins, in January 1945, the U.S. had arrived late for two European wars, between which it had been isolationist and arbitrary over the issue of the war debts.[5] When the U.S. did intervene, it insisted on dominating its supposed allies. One example of such arrogance was Roosevelt's invitation to de Gaulle to meet him in Algiers. This was the thinking that lay behind de Gaulle's later belief that in a nuclear age the U.S. would not sacrifice New York to save Paris. Logically de Gaulle sought European allies and used them to increase French independence of the U.S. or to gain leverage over the U.S. The second of these complemented the first and contradicts the facile notion that de Gaulle merely wanted the U.S. to "go home."

The goal of Franco-German reconciliation was already present in de Gaulle's thought in 1945. Significantly it was raised during his conversation with Roosevelt's envoy. The hapless Hopkins tried to please de Gaulle by informing him that the American position on the Rhine resembled France's. De Gaulle replied that the U.S. had no business taking a position on the Rhine. France and Germany must find the solution: "Toutes deux l'avaient longtemps cherché l'une contre l'autre. Demain elles la découvrirait, peut-etre, en s'associant."[6]

The Poincaré approach (named for the interwar statesman who believed in taking a tough line with Germany and in using force if necessary) jostled in de Gaulle's thinking with a distinction between the Nazi regime and the German people whom he admired, not least because of the courage shown by soldiers and civilians alike in the face of defeat. As he toured the rubble of German cities, he began to think that the Poincaré approach was no longer necessary. He also admitted that the destruction of the German people was not in Europe's interest. He reformulated his vision of Europe to exclude the USSR and, implicitly, to include a German state: France would bring together the states that bordered on the Rhine, the Alps and the Pyrenees (presumably including Franco's Spain?). They would play an intermediary role between the Soviet and Anglo-Saxon camps.[7] It is not too much to say that the Franco-German relationship was born as a way to expand the power of the French state against Washington as much as against Moscow.

Atlanticist Germans

By the time de Gaulle came back to power in 1958, the Franco-German relationship had acquired a clear economic form but it was politically hazy. From the European Coal and Steel Community (ECSC) France had gained secure access to German coal for its steel industry. From the negotiations that culminated in the creation of the European Economic Community (EEC), France had gained an outlet for its agricultural surplus. Germany's economic gains from the ECSC were less tangible, although via the EEC the French market was opened to its industrial products.

Politically, the reconciliation that de Gaulle had foreseen was furthered by the ECSC which gave France a measure of control over the industries that had served the German war machine. Entwining the two economies substituted the Briand method (called after the interwar statesman who believed in Franco-German reconciliation) for the Poincaré method: France did not keep Germany in chains but instead embraced its ally so tightly as to enmesh it. Reconciliation did not exclude a measure of control. If this expanded the power of the French state, the fledgling German state gained legitimacy from *Gleichberechtigung* or equal treatment. It also learned to control itself. Both nation-states were able to grow stronger by working together. But on East-West relations Adenauer looked first to the U.S. for its military power, while Franco-German cooperation had been set back by the EDC.

There were several lessons to be drawn from the state of Franco-German relations in 1958. Firstly, economics provided better terrain for agreement than politics. There were clashes here too: Germany looked worldwide and the percentage of its exports that went to advanced countries outside the EC was higher than the French percentage.[8] Germany wanted a low external tariff, France a higher one. But on agriculture, the positions were reversed: France wanted the price of grain fixed lower so that its farmers could outsell German farmers in their own market. So there was room for compromise. The problems that would stem from cooperation, such as coordination of macroeconomic policies and monetary union, were decades away.

In politics there were, alongside the agreements to avoid a fourth Franco-German war and to resist the military threat from the USSR, two immediate disagreements. The first was that federalist West Germany was willing to sacrifice sovereignty to a supranational, united Europe, whereas Jacobin-Bonapartist France was not. The second was Germany's tenacious Atlanticism that clashed with the French determination, reinforced by the Suez expedition, to gain more autonomy from the U.S.

These differing views spilled over into domestic politics. In Germany Kurt Schumacher worried that locking the BRD into a united

Western Europe meant giving up whatever hope of reunification there might be. After him the SPD looked more to Scandinavia or Britain than to France. Ludwig Erhard was the spokesman within the Christian Democrats for the view that Germany had worldwide economic interests, while Adenauer was more sensitive to the importance of the BRD taking its place among the Western European nations, of which France was the most important. Perhaps the Adenauer-Erhard split was more important than the SPD-CDU conflict. Arguably, Helmut Kohl faced the same choice after he won the GDR elections in March 1990: should Germany seek out its own path or should it assume that its path would lead to greater European unity? But the terms in which the question was posed were very different in the 1950s. Possessing only the building blocks of a state, Adenauer saw no contradiction between the future German state and an integrated Western Europe as well as an Atlantic Alliance.

Quite the reverse, the Soviet threat could only be met by a strong Europe, which could not be constructed without Germany. Germany could not rearm unless it was free to chose rearmament. In the ECSC (European Coal and Steel Community), Adenauer gave up a control over German heavy industry which he never really possessed, in return for which he gained a partial control via the six-nation community. Adenauer won the argument with Erhard because of the economic miracle with which Erhard has been credited. Adenauer was mortally afraid of being dubbed the "Allies' Chancellor," but his choice of European unity and the Western Alliance was reinforced by high living standards. There remained the tightrope that Adenauer had to walk between the U.S. and France. But he was consistent both in trying to reconcile the two and in giving priority—at least until 1963—to the U.S.

In France opinion was sharply divided. The Communists were generally opposed to cooperation with Germany, while the Socialists and what one might (borrowing René Rémond's method of distinguishing three rightwing traditions: Legitimist, Orléanist, and Bonapartist) call the Orléanist family, represented in the 1970s by Valéry Giscard d'Estaing, were pro-German. There remained de Gaulle.

De Gaulle's supposedly ambiguous legacy was apparent in the 1993 Maastricht referendum. Two thirds of his party (Rassemblement pour la république, or *RPR*) voted no under the guidance of Charles Pasqua and Philippe Séguin, while one third followed the RPR leader, Jacques Chirac, into the yes camp. The ambiguity resulted from de Gaulle's blend of unchanging goals to be reached by a dazzlingly varied array of tactics. In 1958, as in 1945, he wished to enhance the role of the French state, using Germany and Europe where he could.

De Gaulle began negotiating with the U.S. on the base of his "memorandum"[9] to gain more leverage for France in NATO. At the same time he held his first meeting with Adenauer in September 1958 and set about converting Germany to his vision of Europe. Displeased, although unsurprised by the American refusal to allow France what he considered its fair share of power, de Gaulle concentrated on Europe and added a second prong to his assault with the Fouché Plan.

In contrast with the dominant but ineffectual supranationalism of the EEC Commission, de Gaulle proposed regular meetings among national governments to achieve broad political agreements. Power was to remain in the national capitals, the national parliaments were to play a role, whereas there was to be no elected EC parliament and Brussels was to be staffed by civil servants on loan from their home capitals. As the debate about the Fouchet Plan went on, it became increasingly obvious that the agreements reached would not be gratifying to the U.S.

The Plan was defeated by Atlanticist countries like the Netherlands but by then de Gaulle had found a substitute for it in the Franco-German treaty. He had deployed the tactic of seduction in his many meetings with Adenauer. By giving Franco-German economic cooperation a political structure, de Gaulle offered the BRD legitimacy as a European state. By supporting Adenauer over Berlin, when both Macmillan and Kennedy faltered, de Gaulle presented the Franco-German relationship as authentically European.

The Treaty, which de Gaulle presented to Adenauer after vetoing British entry to the EEC—a veto that was entirely consistent with the Treaty—called for regular meetings between the two governments to discuss economic and security issues. The joint positions reached would then be taken into other fora like NATO.[10]

The continuity with de Gaulle's revised view of Germany in 1945 was apparent. Bound to France, the FRG would be unable to harm France. De Gaulle was probably the last French statesman not to fear Germany's economic might. He considered that French military and political power and the strong state institutions he had created in 1958 outweighed German industry. Once more, the domestic reassertion of the state was an integral part of foreign policy: Chirac has had less success in this area. Together—and without Britain—France and Germany would form the core of a bloc situated between the Soviet and Anglo-Saxon blocs, although de Gaulle never set these two in the same category. He stood by the U.S. throughout the Cuban missile crisis.

Yet, de Gaulle did demand that Germany be less Atlanticist and Germany refused. The Bundestag's preamble to the 1963 Treaty subordinated its provisions to Germany's commitments to NATO and, interestingly, to the GATT. Soon after Adenauer ceded power to the Atlanticist, Erhard. The Treaty was now worthless to de Gaulle, who turned away from Germany. He also followed the "empty chair" policy in the EEC and in 1966 pulled France out of the military although not the political structure of NATO.

These are the actions that have given rise to the supposed ambivalence between de Gaulle the European and de Gaulle the nationalist. This is, however, misleading because de Gaulle pursued throughout his life the ideal of a strong, free France. Only when he decided that the EEC and NATO were not helping him realize his goal, did he turn to the tactic of France going its own way. The Phnom-Penh speech and the "Vive le Québec libre" appeal followed. The independent nuclear deterrent, the *force de frappe,* remained French, although it was supposed one day to become a "cornerstone" in the construction of Europe.[11] De Gaulle had over Chirac the advantage that the margin of freedom left to the nation state was greater in the 1960s than it is today.

Two of de Gaulle's propositions about a Franco-German axis have proved correct, while the third is only partially so. De Gaulle was right in switching from the Poincaré to the Briand line and seeing that the best way to control Germany was to draw it into a web of agreements. He was right too that, if there were to be a Europe, it would have to be organized by France and Germany. Britain would not and Italy could not do it. Finally de Gaulle foresaw Europe asserting itself between other blocs. But while he did foresee the collapse of the Soviet system, he did not imagine that the Cold War would be resolved by the collapse of "la Russie éternelle. Nor did he foresee the development of a global economy. The former permitted German Reunification which brought new problems to divide France and Germany. The latter simultaneously forced upon the two countries a degree of economic unity that de Gaulle did not envisage. Would he have supported EMU? Probably not. Still the 1996 reshaping of NATO is very Gaullist.

Chirac and the Franco-German Partnership He Inherited

In the 1995 presidential campaign, Chirac presented himself as de Gaulle's successor. He declared his candidacy at Lille partly because de Gaulle was born there; he was the standard-bearer of the "Gaullist" party, and his main theme was that political will could reshape economic and social reality. Yet Chirac is a very different leader from de Gaulle, while the Franco-German relationship has changed much since the abortive 1963 Treaty.

Having grown looser in de Gaulle's last years, the bond between the two countries was weakened during Georges Pompidou's presidency (1969–74) and enmity returned. For this there was one main reason: the French government now faced the fact of German power. Fear of the *Wehrmacht* had vanished, but the social conflicts of the late 1960s and the monetary disputes of the early 1970s emphasized the FRG's economic strength. Pompidou gambled on high growth to overtake Germany: he achieved growth but at the cost of soaring inflation—7.3 per cent in 1973. When the oil crisis duly arrived, France was in a far weaker economic position than its neighbor.

This was also the moment when the FRG undertook its first bold initiative in foreign policy. Brandt's *Ostpolitik,* although foreshadowed by de Gaulle's opening to Moscow, had greater short-term success. Brandt did not ask the Communist countries to change—other than to permit greater contact with the West, which may in the long run have helped undermine them—and he came bearing gifts. He convinced an at first hesitant FRG public opinion and he was acclaimed abroad. Although he tried to conciliate Pompidou, the French president nurtured the fear—which came true in 1989—that Germany would become the Soviet Empire's prime interlocutor in Western Europe. Pompidou turned for support to Britain, but the possibility of a French-British axis vanished when Edward Heath lost the 1974 elections. The postwar truth that Britain could not or would not play a leading role in the EC was once more vindicated.

Domestic German politics was turbulent in the early years of the Ostpolitik as Brandt faced a strong New Left and a CDU that found itself in opposition for the first time. In this context, policies like the *Rechtsstaat* and the opening to the East were important in establishing the SPD's identity as the governing party of a changing Germany. The Franco-German relationship could not serve this purpose, although Brandt did not neglect it. He knew that without a safe Western base, the opening to the East was impossible. Still this period provides the proof that domestic political change in either country could affect cooperation.

The irony of the Franco-German dispute was that it came just when U.S. leadership was faltering and when a European initiative was needed. Nixon's decisions to separate the dollar from gold and to devalue, while at the same time imposing an import surcharge of 10 percent, sent a clear message that the U.S. was no longer able to carry out its hegemonic role and intended to look after its own national interests.[12] The Europeans were put to the test and they failed it. They failed to establish a stable monetary zone or to unite on a plan which they could then put to the U.S. So the dollar remained the major currency of world trade, although the U.S. allowed it to fluctuate against gold as against other currencies.

The apparent reason for the European failure was that France and Germany held different views on money. The French sought fixed parities; the Germans were more willing to float. But deeper reasons were that the two were pursuing different macroeconomic policies and that the political will was lacking. By 1978 these two obstacles had been removed. President Giscard d'Estaing had opted for austerity, and lower inflation replaced higher growth as the French government's priority. Giscard had not merely established a good working relationship with Chancellor Helmut Schmidt, but he had offered Germany as a model to his countrymen.[13]

Schmidt was now to demonstrate the limits of the power that domestic politics has to weaken the Franco-German relationship. He did so not only by showing that cooperation could be fruitful when the SPD governed Germany but also because he ended up with France as a partner after exhausting other strategies. Firstly, he lost all confidence in the Carter administration. The fiasco of the neutron bomb and Carter's willingness to let the dollar go down rather than pursue energy conservation exasperated Schmidt. Secondly, he could go no further and time was needed before the seeds of Western culture (or Western decadence) could sprout. Finally, as he looked around Europe, Schmidt saw his British comrades grow more anti-European as the transition period after Britain's entry to the EC came to a close, while Italy was immersed in the—to Schmidt—byzantine intricacies of the historic compromise. These factors drove Schmidt into Giscard's arms. The result was the European Monetary System (EMS).

Both Giscard and Schmidt left office before the EMS, launched in 1979, began to work. Not until Mitterrand gave up the Keynesianism of his first two years and re-opted for austerity, now called rigueur, in 1983, did financial markets take the EMS seriously. Once more the need for France and Germany to follow the same macroeconomic policy was underlined. French inflation fell steadily after 1983, and the only further devaluations of the franc were made when Chirac was Prime Minister from 1986 to 1988, as the financial markets still remember.

Mitterrand turned his choice of *rigueur* into a project and one might argue that "Europe" replaced socialism as the goal of his fourteen years in power. He established good working relations with Helmut Kohl. He relaunched the ailing EC at the 1984 Fontainebleau summit and dispatched Jacques Delors to Brussels to look after it. The Single European Act was in part Mitterrand's work. He increased Franco-German defense cooperation without asking Germany to choose between France and the U.S. Indeed Mitterrand won praise from the Reagan administration by his support for NATO's decision to install the Pershing and Cruise missiles. The principle that Franco-German initiatives in security matters needed American blessing was maintained.

Mitterrand viewed the Franco-German partnership in the same way as de Gaulle had done. It was a guarantee against future wars and a pooling of resources that increased the power of the French state. Defense cooperation did not involve sharing control over the *force de frappe,* even if Germany hoped that cooperation would include, or lead to, some consultation before it was used. If the EMS meant accepting the yoke of the *Bundesbank,* then the French government gained domestic power through its capacity to overcome inflation and to redistribute value-added. Abroad, the moves towards a European defense system provided protection against the erratic USSR. This was an area where France led and where its supremacy could counterbalance German industrial power. Via its tie with Germany, France increased its influence in the EC: the twice-yearly Franco-German summits set the agenda for the Council of Ministers meetings. One limit on French and EC power was that the EMS provided no leverage over the dollar. That has remained true, although the drive towards monetary union is inspired in part by the old desire to limit the U.S.'s ability to move the dollar up or down without paying the penalties other countries must pay when they manipulate their currencies.

As the 1980s wore on—even before German reunification— France began to perceive the disadvantages of cooperation. Chief among them was the fixed relationship of the franc and the mark. Since the markets continued to doubt the franc, French interest rates included the risk penalty factor which raised them some two or three percent above German rates. Demographic factors, such as the larger number of young people coming onto the labor market, meant that France needed a higher growth rate than Germany if unemployment were to be held at an acceptable level. There was some evidence that, since France imported machine tools from Germany, it ran a trade deficit with Germany whenever its industry expanded. This brought pressure on the franc, pushed up interest rates and cut off expansion.[14]

The solution was to persuade Germany to reduce its interest rates and the Mitterrand government tried in 1988. Jealous of its independence and conscious that its charter imposed on it no responsibilities towards foreign countries, the *Bundesbank* refused. France tried without avail to work through the Franco-German economic council set up by the 1963 Treaty. This inability to influence Germany came precisely when Mikhail Gorbachev's peace campaign was creating the (erroneous) impression that security problems were fading away and with them the importance of France's independent deterrent and its role as the strongest military power in continental Western Europe.

The impact of German reunification must be set in this context. Mitterrand's trip to Kiev to meet Gorbachev proved as futile as his attempts to prop up some sort of revamped GDR government.[15] Kohl undertook the task of reunification without consulting his EC partners and Gorbachev dealt with him directly. Kohl saw his chance and seized it before it could vanish. He had U.S. support and could—provided he was successful—dispense with Europeans who wanted to play the role of guarantors. French public opinion was not disturbed: its elites had told it that Germany should be reunited.[16] Those elites, however, were appalled that some forty years of embracing Germany had not enmeshed it. The winter of 1989–90 marks the start of Mitterrand's decline.

In considering his options Mitterrand came up against a problem that de Gaulle had not had to face. The bond with Germany and with the EC in general, as well as the worldwide assembly line and the free, rapid movement of capital, harbingers of the global economy, had internationalized the nation-state. Not that the state had lost all power, but its role was to bargain on behalf of its citizens in fora like the EC or the GATT. It was difficult for Mitterrand to withdraw from the partnership with Germany. Moreover, the French political class had committed its prestige to the EMS and to the thesis that France increased its power via its cooperation with Germany. Finally, the two countries were bound by trade; each was the other's leading partner. Mitterrand had no option but to press ahead.

French estimates of French power change more rapidly and more drastically than the power itself. They are perception rather than reality and in the spring of 1990 France was stronger than it thought. Kohl could strike out on his own to obtain Reunification but he could not allow it to be the cause of a lasting break with France and the EC. So, after winning the GDR elections in March 1990, he turned back to Mitterrand. The price Germany had to pay for reunification was Economic and Monetary Union (EMU). This was an example of how France sought to solve its problems by greater integration rather than by withdrawal. Monetary union would, theoretically, take away the risk penalty factor. It would also give France one vote and the opportunity to form alliances in a future European Central Bank. Put crudely, it was a way to gain a measure of power over the *Bundesbank*.

So, from the outset, monetary union, seen as the latest phase of the Franco-German relationship, was controversial in Germany. The *Bundesbank* insisted on conditions that were unsuited to the economic circumstances of the 1990s and that have proved arduous even to Germany. Segments of the press, notably *Der Spiegel,* were scathing about French motives for monetary union and about the entire French project of using Germany and Europe to maintain *grandeur.* Public opinion data suggest that the more ordinary Germans learned about monetary union, the less they liked it. One could—and still can— imagine an élite-populist alliance gathering around the refusal to give up the mark. But there had to be a link between the two segments and the SPD, perhaps mindful of how it had mismanaged reunification, was reluctant to provide it.

Kohl wrapped himself in Adenauer's greatcoat and maintained that no German state could exist outside of a united Europe. This was obviously much less true than in the 1950s and there was no very obvious reason why Germany should regard monetary union as the essential ingredient in European unity. Still Kohl's domestic position grew stronger in the years after reunification, partly because other leaders lost power: Thatcher in 1990, Andreotti in 1992, and Mitterrand in 1995. By now Kohl had been in power for thirteen years and had no plans to resign.

The Maastricht Treaty, which emerged from the Council of Ministers meeting of December 1991, represented, as usual, a Franco-German compromise but it was a French rather than a German document. Germany would give up the mark, even if it imposed draconian conditions of entry to the EMU. Some progress was made toward a common foreign and security policy. The Iraqi War had disposed of the facile notion that defense issues were destined to fade away. Saddam Hussein had revealed both the importance of the French and British forces and the general European disarray. The EC countries could not act together, while even Britain and France were dependent on the U.S. for advanced information technology.

Franco-German military cooperation had moved forward with the creation of the Eurocorps and the revival of the Western European Union (WEU). But this triggered the old problem of American susceptibility about NATO. The Maastricht meeting was preceded by a clash between the Bush administration, which wanted the WEU to be an integral part of NATO, and the Mitterrand government, that adopted the Gaullist view of a Europe able to defend itself and, hence, saw the WEU as the military arm of the EC. The Maastricht Treaty devised the non-solution of ambiguous wording, which probably suited Germany. In January 1992 Mitterrand half-offered to share the *force de frappe* with the other Europeans but he probably wanted a less Atlanticist WEU. Anyway, it is hard to imagine a nuclear deterrent with several fingers on its trigger and the problem of Europeanizing the *force de frappe* remains.

On the internal organization of the EC, now to be baptized the EU (European Union), France permitted scant deviance from the Gaullist "Europe of the Fatherlands" approach. The question remained, however, whether this was real: whether the bargaining state was a state in de Gaulle's sense of the term. The social clauses of the Treaty offered the British a pretext to marginalize themselves. Franco-German hegemony in the EU was confirmed.

Yet the French referendum on the Treaty produced the narrowest of victories for the yes camp—51-49 percent. Cities, rich regions, and middle-class voters were generally favorable, while blue-collar voters and the countryside said no. The referendum was a warning to Jacques Chirac and a triumph for Philippe Séguin, the voice of popular, nationalist Gaullism. To what extent was this a vote against the Franco-German relationship? In all probability, the large no vote was a protest less against Germany than against a cluster of problems that were linked to varying degrees with Maastricht, the German connection, and the EU. The most important was unemployment, which had risen steadily since 1990. The reasons run from demography via bad job training to the strong franc and high interest rates. These last were associated with the Maastricht criteria for monetary union. Economic integration was less easy than in the 1950s.

The Franco-German relationship had changed in ways that seemed unfavorable to France and that damaged both the ruling Parti socialiste (PS) and Mitterrand himself. It was difficult to argue that cooperation increased the power of the French state, which was weakened internally by unemployment and by the sporadic waves of protest that characterize France. The Balladur government was no more able to influence German economic policy, as was demonstrated in August 1993 when the Bundesbank's decision not to lower interest rates precipitated a run on the franc and the end of the narrow bands in the EMS. The collapse of the Soviet Empire removed one spur to cooperation. Germany and France initially backed different sides in the Yugoslav civil war. Germany was more enthusiastic about EU expansion to the Central European countries, while France looked more to the Mediterranean. But the main issue was that France was locked into an economic system that forced it to deflate and left it with an unacceptable unemployment rate of 12 percent.

However, the problem was not, as French elites had feared in 1989, that a reunited Germany was too strong. Rather Germany was too weak to respond to the many demands made on it. The GDR economy, damaged by the replacement of its currency by the FRG's mark, required more aid and time than was at first thought. In a tougher world economy West German labor costs became prohibitively high. Voices from abroad called on Germany to play a greater role in foreign and security affairs and then castigated it when it sided with Croatia. As usual, France was less weak than it feared because Germany was less strong than France feared. While this new weaker Germany might prove a less efficient partner, it was almost certain to be faithful. It simply could not afford to break with its enemy-rival-friend.

This was the setting in which Jacques Chirac took over French responsibility for the Franco-German relationship. What views, talents, and defects did he bring to his task? Chirac had inherited the nationalist stand in Gaullism and his formative, political years were Pompidou's presidency when the Franco-German relationship was faring badly. As Minister of Agriculture, he had furious arguments with his German counterpart about the green currencies. When Chirac became leader of the Gaullist party in 1976, the logic of Giscard's Europeanism strengthened his nationalism. But in the 1979 direct elections to the European Parliament, his party ran on a nationalist platform and was defeated by Giscard's party.[17]

Chirac has never forgotten this. In the TV interview of October 26, 1995, which marked his switch of priorities, he declared himself "a realistic European." He accepts that France needs Europe and especially Germany if it is to influence the global economy. By temperament Chirac sees little that is good outside the hexagon. His second brush with German leaders turned out like his first. Outraged at the U.S.'s willingness, expressed at the Reykjavik meeting of autumn 1986, to negotiate away nuclear weapons that were defending Western Europe, Chirac called on the Kohl government to form a military arrangement with France. The French nuclear deterrent was virtually to replace the medium-range NATO missiles. However, the Atlanticists and the disarmers in Germany joined forces to kill the proposal. Mitterrand lent the Germans a hand and was rewarded when Bonn supported him against Chirac in the 1988 presidential elections. So Chirac had few credentials as an advocate of Franco-German cooperation. His evolution would demonstrate, however, the solid, objective reasons for the tie to persist.

President Chirac: From Integrating the Excluded to Re-embracing the Germans

It may appear surprising that Chirac won the presidential race in 1995. He had made two previous attempts and had failed either to reach 20 percent or to enter the second round. Throughout the autumn 1994, he ran at least 15 points behind Edouard Balladur in the polls and as late as mid-January 1995 he had 14 percent of the vote to the Prime Minister's 27 percent. Chirac was able to overtake Balladur for three reasons. The first was that Balladur began to campaign, an activity for which he has no talent. The second was that, after two years of rewarding Balladur for telling the truth about how little a national government could do, the electorate grew weary and turned to a man who could be relied on to do something, even if no one knew what. The third reason was that Chirac broke through with his discourse of a social fracture which the republican state could mend.[18]

Already in 1993 the Gaullists had won the parliamentary elections because they incarnated the activist state better than the *Union pour la démocratie française* (UDF) or than the discredited Socialists who had allowed unemployment to rise so steeply. Now Chirac denounced the weakening of the political will, which had allowed "the mad reign of money."[19] Adopting the language of left-wing Gaullism, Chirac criticized casino capitalism and financial speculation. He denied that the global market could run itself and reiterated his willingness to use state power in order to combat exclusion. The nation was still alive and well, even if Mitterrand and Balladur had neglected it. The discourse of exclusion—a term used generically to cover the unemployed, the poor, the homeless—was an implicit admission that the post-1983 policy of the strong franc and the tie with Germany had damaged French society.

At the outset of the campaign, Chirac called for a referendum on monetary union. It would have been logical to advocate a switch of policy to the view represented by Séguin, who was supporting him against Balladur. Séguin favored lower interest rates and letting the franc float at the cost of a break with Germany. Chirac flirted with these views and he showed his nationalism when he suggested renegotiating the Schengen agreement. But, as his chances of winning the election increased, he grew increasingly orthodox on the Franco-German relationship.

He thus won the election—taking 43 percent of the working-class vote—on a populist platform which involved more state spending but he refused to break with the constraints imposed by French commitments to Europe. This ambiguity would have to be resolved after the election, not that one more change of mind meant much to a politician whose only consistent traits were the speed with which he switched his positions and the energy with which he defended each of them. Still a political bill would be sent for this flagrant contradiction although the unfortunate Alain Juppé had to pay the largest part.[20]

Chirac began with a feeble attempt to fulfill his promises to integrate the excluded. He inaugurated the *Contrat initiative-emploi (CIE)*: a series of incentives to employers to hire the longterm unemployed. But the contract was not very different from existing plans to fight unemployment. Moreover it was to be financed by an increase in the VAT from 18.6 to 20.6 percent, which cut consumption and fell most heavily on the poor. Other measures were mostly symbolic: convincing the G7 to set unemployment on its agenda or inserting social issues into the EU's intergovernmental conferences. Paradoxically their symbolism sent the message that the French state could not act on its own to reduce unemployment.

Although Chirac met Helmut Kohl directly after his election, this first period was marked by a certain coolness in the Franco-German relationship. Chirac declared it necessary but not sufficient and added that there could be no Europe without Britain. But, although Britain is an obvious partner for France on defense issues where progress has indeed been made, the Conservative government's euroscepticism, divisions and sheer weakness rendered it almost worthless as an ally. Already by August 1985, Chirac was affirming that Cold War bipolarity had given way to a multipolar world; that the EU would be one of the two or three most important blocs and that leadership of the EU could come only from France and Germany.[21] This restated the view of the Franco-German relationship propounded by de Gaulle and Mitterrand. It suited Germany which had and has no desire to play the role of solitary leader.

As usual action could not follow until France and Germany adopted the same macroeconomic policy. Here too the shift was not long in coming. On October 26, Chirac went on TV to declare that "he had underestimated the gravity of the problem" posed by government spending. Priority must be given to reducing the deficit and there would be two years of austerity. Chirac resorted to Gaullist language to explain that "national independence" demanded that the deficit be mastered. As for the excluded, the only way to create jobs was to liberate resources for private investment.[22]

Chirac was resorting to orthodox economics. He announced plans to cut the deficit from above five to three percent of GDP by 1997. In the years 1990–94 the deficit had risen from 2 to 6 percent of GDP and the debt from 35 to 49 percent of GDP.[23] Part of the increase stemmed from unemployment which had gone up from 9 to 12.5 percent during the same period. Cutting the deficit, said President Chirac, would bring down interest rates, enabling the private sector, especially the small companies to expand and create jobs. There was no other way: this was *la pensée unique*.

Followers of Philippe Séguin pointed out that during these four years German reunification had been paid for with inadequate tax increases and borrowed money. To avoid inflation, the *Bundesbank* had raised interest rates. Since France—and other EU countries—had to follow suit, unemployment had risen and governments, whether of the left or the right, had resorted to palliatives in the form of higher benefits. The solution was to cut not the deficit but the tie with Germany; there were other roads.

Chirac had come to the opposite conclusion. Invoking his realism, he re-endorsed the Franco-German relationship and went further. He expressed support for enlargement to include the whole continent, which was a way of saying he would support Germany's aim of obtaining EU membership for Hungary, Poland and the Czech Republic. In a government reshuffle Chirac brought in Balladur supporters who believed in deficit cutting and the tie with Germany.

When Prime Minister Juppé announced cuts in social security in November 1995, massive strikes brought Paris to a halt. Significantly, the Parisians blamed the inconvenience they suffered on the government rather than on the strikers. The social security fund, financed mostly out of employer-employee contributions, had its own deficit, which Juppé planned to eliminate by the end of 1997. One way was to demand forty years of contributions from public sector employees rather than thirty-seven and a half years. Another was to terminate the privileges enjoyed by groups like railway men. These measures were accompanied by a partial wage freeze in the public sector.

The Prime Minister demonstrated an inability to communicate with ordinary people that lent credence to the harshest criticisms of l'ENA. It seemed the traditional French clash between a remote, authoritarian government and an anarchist-corporatist segment of the population. However, the traditional conclusion, which consisted of a back down by the government and a return to the status quo, did not take place. Certainly Juppé made concessions, especially to the railway men. But he did not capitulate or change policy and the strikes were not resumed after the Christmas break.

In the first half of 1996 domestic politics featured an unpopular Prime Minister protecting an unpopular President who was determined to impose an economic policy that was the antithesis of the policy on which he had campaigned. Unlike the de Gaulle of 1958, Chirac had not strengthened the state. His parliamentary majority transmitted the grassroots' anger but could not placate it. By July 1996 Chirac's approval rating was down at 42 percent, while Juppé's stood at 34 percent.[24] In his Bastille Day address Chirac admitted that the country was enveloped in massive uncertainty.[25] In a flash of his old populism he blamed the banks for high interest rates. In August the government took tough measures against illegal immigrants, which sent Chirac and Juppé up in the polls. But with unemployment at 12.5 percent, the media talked of little but the second difficult autumn. One feels that the tide of words about the social disturbances was designed to exorcise them.

Unsurprisingly, Chirac was spending much time abroad. One could divide his foreign policy into two segments: European and non-European. But this would be misleading because the non-European ventures are designed to retain a world role which gives France greater influence in Europe. Similarly, France's leading role in the EU enables it to exert an influence worldwide.

Chirac made two trips to Africa and one to the Middle East. In Africa he offered support to another excluded group and spread the news that there would indeed be French help but not for undemocratic and wasteful governments. The Middle East journey was to reassert a French presence that had been overshadowed by the U.S. since the Gulf War and to sketch a policy towards Iraq and Iran that differs from the American policy. The difference became clear when President Clinton launched the missile strike against Iraq in September 1996. The Chirac government decided that French planes would patrol only the old no-go zone and not the expanded, larger one. France was renewing its "kind" approach which aims eventually at establishing dialogue with all Arab regimes.

In Europe, Chirac needed to take the initiative in order to convince his protesting citizens that there was a reward for their austerity. However his first action, which was to resume nuclear testing, was an assertion of state power in a classic Gaullist manner: the *force de frappe* remained the badge of French independence. The resumption of testing encountered understanding from Britain, itself a nuclear power. It was greeted with reluctant tolerance from the German government, which had to confront its relatively strong Green movement. It faced the outright opposition of Italy which voted in the UN to condemn the tests. France responded to Italy by canceling a proposed summit between Chirac and Dini and by renewing its criticisms of Italy's devaluation of the lira.

This was a harsh reaction by France. In part it may be explained by Chirac's temperament, but it was a sign that the French government had underrated opposition to its tests. It tried to meet criticism by renewing Mitterrand's half-offer that the French deterrent could become the core of a European defense system.[26]

But this time the half-offer was part of a serious debate about European defense and its relationship to NATO. There were three differences between this debate and the 1991 argument. The Clinton administration did not, like the Bush administration, see the U.S. as a lone superpower, one of whose duties was to dominate NATO. Although sporadic and erratic in its ventures into European affairs, as it demonstrated in Northern Ireland, the Clinton administration was aware that the U.S. was overburdened and it was willing to help the Europeans help themselves. Clinton himself grew more interested in foreign affairs as his term of office went on and he was not averse to demonstrating to the Europeans that the U.S. could solve their problems better than they could. The U.S. initiative in Bosnia offers an example. However, the European record in Bosnia had been abysmal until Chirac initiated a bolder policy, declaring that France would play a leading role in the attempt to open a safe road to Sarajevo. Such progress as has been made in Bosnia is the result of Franco- (and Anglo-) American cooperation and without Chirac's initiative the U.S. might not have moved.

The second difference was that Chirac's view of the U.S.'s role in NATO was not Mitterrand's. Where his predecessor was suspicious of every American move, Chirac and his advisors were convinced that the end of the Cold War meant the end of a U.S. dominated NATO. Clinton had been elected to turn the U.S. government inward and concentrate on domestic, economic issues. In any case the bipolar universe was giving way to a unified global economy with several nerve centers. To survive, NATO would have to deconstruct itself. No longer did it exist to defend against one well-defined enemy: its new tasks would be peace-making and peace-keeping operations; intervening in many different areas, such as the Middle East, North Africa and Central Europe; it would defend its members against less mighty but more varied threats than had been posed by the USSR. In these circumstances, so the French Right argued, NATO must become more flexible, divide up responsibility on a geographical basis and be organized around a group of leading countries.[27] De Gaulle had successfully resisted U.S. domination; now the time had come for France to lead Europe into a shared hegemony.

The third difference was that Germany was not being asked to chose between Gaullism and Atlanticism. In February 1996 Kohl joined Chirac in calling for a more European NATO. The Maastricht ambiguity was to be resolved by making the WEU an integral part both of the EU and of NATO. At a NATO meeting in June, the U.S. agreed that NATO structures, which are essentially American structures, may be used by the European countries with U.S. permission but without U.S. participation. In turn this permits a French return to NATO's military organization.

This arrangement represents a triumph for the Franco-German relationship. The reshaped WEU has grown out of the Bold Sparrow exercise and the Franco-German corps which Mitterrand and a more reluctant Kohl organized in the years after 1983. If this formula suits Germany by providing it with a safe framework within which to play its proper role in European defense, it offers France a position of leadership. This makes the subordinate role France plays in monetary affairs more palatable to its elites. Once more both countries gain strength by cooperating. Finally, if the new agreement improves Franco-British defense cooperation, this will not turn Britain into a leader of the EU. It will, however, make France a more attractive ally for Germany.

The summer of 1996 saw important developments in EU collaboration to produce armaments. In July, Britain disregarded American bids and chose British Aerospace along with Matra to manufacture a new missile. Britain also decided to join in a Franco-German tank project. The information satellites Hélios 2 and Horus are being built by a consortium of German, French, Italian and Spanish companies. As if to remind us that a strong Europe is primarily a theater for French power, Chirac restricted British Aerospace's role in Matra's takeover of the armaments segment of Thompson.[28]

Much remains to be done before de Gaulle's vision of a Europe that could defend itself is realized. The Chirac government is no exception to the rule that almost all contemporary governments are cutting defense spending. The organization of the decentered NATO and the precise roles of the various countries have yet to be arranged. The creation of a Common European Foreign and Security Policy (CFSP), of which the WEU would be the military arm, lags much further behind.[29] It is still too soon to see the *force de frappe* become the cornerstone of European defense.

It is also unfortunate that Chirac's success in using the Franco-German partnership to enhance France's role in security issues in no way compensates the voters for the austerity imposed in the name of a common currency. Candidate Chirac declared that the paypacket was no enemy of employment and French economic recovery is held back by a lack of demand. The Ministry of Finance's growth estimate for 1997 has been revised downward from 2.5-2.8 percent to 2.25-2.5 percent, but even the lower figure seems high. Nor is it certain that France will meet the Maastricht requirements; independent analysts are predicting a 3.5-4 percent deficit for 1997.[30] The markets doubt whether France can or will persist with austerity. This puts pressure on the franc and makes it more difficult to persist.

Another reason for French woes is the travail of the German economy, which has grown weaker in the mid-1990s. The *Bundesbank* complains that Germany cannot at present meet the Maastricht criterion; the deficit is around 4 percent and the debt is above 60 percent of GDP. But the real trouble is that the ex-GDR is proving to be a burden in some respects comparable to the *Mezzogiorno*. In turn this makes the strong mark less of an asset. *Modell Deutschland* is no more. How much longer will the *Bundesbank* and the financial markets keep its ghost alive?

Both Germany and France suffer from currencies that are overvalued against the dollar and against the devalued lira and pound. Both economies drift along with no hope of rapid recovery. Meanwhile the common currency, to be introduced in distant 1999, offers uncertainties of its own. It should be accompanied by changes in tax-structure and improved flexibility of labor but these have yet to be worked out. How will monetary discipline be enforced and what will be the relationship between what is now known in Brussels as the EMS1 and the EMS2 group? Will the euro be a strong or a weak currency and will it finally give Europe some independence from the dollar? That would make the pain that EU members have undergone worthwhile. Economic disputes with the U.S. are likely to increase, while the chances of improved relations in the security field have diminished as Clinton's interest in the outside world has grown.

Chirac has recently gone back to the Gaullist origins of Franco-German cooperation. The Franco-German-led Europe will be able to hold its own with the U.S. in the future debates about money and by its larger role in NATO; it will bring about a reconciliation with Russia.[31] De Gaulle's vision of France emerging as leader of a European bloc between Russia and the Anglo-Saxons is about to be realized. At least that is what the excluded will be told.

Chirac is right to cling to the Franco-German relationship because he has no viable alternatives. To give up the fixed parity with the mark would be to risk a savage attack by the markets, while the jobs created might be few and fleeting. But monetary union, while remaining a long-term solution, has become a problem in its own right. Its installation is taking too long and it has weakened the French government. The Franco-German relationship needs a grand initiative. An immediate introduction of the common currency? A joint devaluation? Neither is likely but without some vision of the promised land, France and Germany are left struggling in the desert.

A Difficult Autumn

Since the main body of this paper was completed in September 1996 there has been much activity in the Franco-German relationship.

No promised land has been sighted on the horizon much less reached and there is little reason to revise the conclusions drawn above. But there have been significant developments such as the Intergovernmental Conference (IGC) and another trip by Chirac to the Middle East. Moreover, the role played in the Franco-German relationship by Italy was highlighted by the Chirac-Prodi clash in September-October. Since this theme was not discussed in the main body of the paper, it may be useful to treat it at some length here. In turn, the contemporary state of Franco-Italian relations must be set in the context of other developments.

Throughout the long march towards European unity Italy has sought to be in the forefront but not to lead. It has accepted France and Germany as the countries that took the initiatives, but has tried to keep up with them. Italy has had few other choices: its domestic political weakness has prevented it from bidding for leadership, the option of forming a Mediterranean bloc within the EU contains the risk of being confined to the second division, while the attempt to form an alliance with Britain over the EMS did not work.[32] Italy and Britain did cooperate in 1991 on the restructuring of NATO where they formed an Atlanticist bloc to support Bush's view. Left to themselves, they have been less able to cooperate.

Although Italy has had to confront the massive influence of the Franco-German alliance, it has evolved various strategies to assure its own European role. The first is to issue declarations of fervent Europeanism at any and every moment. Such outbursts usually contain the boast that Italy was a founding member of the EC. In general, Italy's enthusiasm meshes well with Germany's traditional policy of seeking a federal Europe and official statements made by German government officials about Italy have usually been favorable. Off-the-record comments have been and are very different.

The Italy-France relationship has been more complex. Often France helps Italy and seeks its support in the dialogue-struggle with Germany. As early as the founding of the Coal and Steel Community, France, in order to make it easier for Italy to join, offered access to Algerian iron-ore, although France was trying to keep Algeria outside the pool. In the Winter of 1989–1990, Mitterrand enlisted Andreotti's support in the bid to keep some control over Kohl's dealings with Gorbachev and to exact pledges of German commitment to the EC.

Yet Italy's reputation for unreliable behavior[33] has also led France, in situations where it is struggling to keep pace with Germany, to abandon its so-called Latin sister. Here again, the EMS provides an example. Italy would have preferred the basket to the grid formula and hoped initially that France would persuade Germany to accept it. But Giscard d'Estaing could not win over a Helmut Schmidt who was fighting his own battle to persuade the *Bundesbank* to accept any kind of EMS. Since the grid offered the mark more protection against spendthrift neighbors than the basket did, Schmidt held out for the grid. Giscard accepted, obtaining only minor concessions. Italy eventually accepted too, after obtaining financial help from the EC and after strong pressure was placed on Prime Minister Andreotti by Schmidt and Giscard.[34]

The clash of 1996 offered parallels, although it was also different. The Prodi-Chirac clash occurred directly after the Italian government had presented its budget which contained austerity measures taken in order to enter the first group of countries that were to fuse their currencies. On September 30, Chirac, who was, significantly, addressing a group of textile manufacturers, declared that he did not believe Italy would be able to cut its deficit to the Maastricht limit of three percent. The enraged Prodi hauled in the French ambassador and the forthcoming French-Italian summit in Naples seemed at risk.

Chirac backed down, praised the courage of Prodi's budget and the summit took place with the usual diplomatic smiles. The dispute was, however, not settled. On the French side, the memory of a devaluation that had taken the lira from 233 to the franc in 1992 to 295 to the franc in 1996 and had, according to French businessmen, given Italy an unfair competitive advantage, still rankled. Moreover, it suggested the dangers associated with monetary union. If Italy joined, what guarantee was there that it would not, once membership was assured, abandon austerity? The laxity of the 1994 Berlusconi government was not encouraging. Italy's presence would also encourage the international financial markets to attack the euro. Finally, France wanted Italy to enter, if at all, at an exchange rate of approximately L 850 to the mark (which seemed absurd), whereas Italian industrialists talked of L1150 (which seemed utopian).[35]

Conversely, France did not want Italy left outside the first group and free to devalue. A possible solution was to construct a second group outside the central core of members. These countries would pledge to keep their currencies at a fixed rate against the euro and would move into the first group once they had satisfied the Maastricht requirements.[36] Such a solution was entirely unacceptable to the Prodi government, which would have imposed austerity merely to enter the European Second Division.

As in 1978, France decided it could not profit from an alliance with Italy. Among its Mediterranean neighbors, Spain had more to offer: its security policies were closer to France's and its determination to enter the first group of monetary union was just as great as Italy's. Like Giscard, Chirac had to assure not just Helmut Kohl but the skeptical *Bundesbank* that France was trustworthy. So, Italy became a liability rather than an asset.

There is no reason to regard the Autumn clash as the mark of a decisive change in Franco-Italian relations. There will surely be future issues where it would suit France to have Italy as an ally. In the meantime, Helmut Kohl intervened with a kind word for the Prodi government's austerity policy, although he has to be cautious with his support which might increase German doubts about monetary union.

This raises the questions of German policy toward Italy, France, and the EU. Although Kohl has reaffirmed the Adenauer tradition of rooting the German state in a united Europe, the vision of a federalist, supranational Europe is fading in Germany. This is partly because of the rediscovery of the country, Germany. The "Ossis" have less interest in Europe, if only because all their energy is spent rooting themselves in the new Germany. Nor can German politicians avoid noticing that their counterparts in most other European countries show scant zeal for surrendering national sovereignty.

This fading federalism does not affect Franco-German cooperation because French politicians show no zeal whatever for surrendering
sovereignty. Germany has dragged France into supporting Eastern
expansion of the EU and is following France down the road of a
Common Foreign and Security Policy. But progress on this issue at
the Intergovernmental Conference has, at least as yet, been slow. The
Dublin summit saw no agreement on appointing a spokesman or a
chairman for European foreign policy with a staff to support him.
Discarding the veto seems unlikely.[37] Progress on institutional reform,
where British obstinacy has, as so often, suited other countries well,
is even slower. France and Germany have committed themselves to
"strengthened cooperation"[38] in an EU of variable speeds. It is not
yet clear which forms the cooperation will take.

Jacques Attali has expressed the recurrent French fear of being
overwhelmed by Germany, which is creating a *Zollverein* through
monetary union while refusing any political input into such issues as
the euro's value against the dollar. EU expansion eastward can only
increase German power, which leads Attali to conclude that France
has no vision of where it is heading.[39] As I have already argued, such
outbursts of pessimism are an integral part of French political culture.
In particular, the assumption that Germany does possess a clear vision
of where it is heading may be erroneous.

The German political system is overloaded: its government too
has spent the Autumn debating how to cut public spending; there is
friction in the CDU-FDP coalition and even within the CDU, where
Norbert Blum, a longstanding ally of Kohl, defends the welfare state.[40]
Fear that German industry is pricing itself out of world markets
remains, and at the end of 1996 unemployment was running at over
11 percent. The view that Germany needs radical action to cut social
spending and improve competitiveness has grown. Is Kohl the man
to undertake this task? His position is deteriorating, and Wolfgang
Schäuble has let it be known that he is interested in becoming chancellor. More important, the forces that oppose or seek to delay monetary
union have found a champion in the SPD prime minister of Saxony,
Gerhard Schröder.[41]

It is often said that Kohl is the last German leader to care deeply about France. But our analysis tends to suggest that whoever holds power in Germany comes around to the importance of the French connection. This does not mean the relationship is as vital or as controversial as it is to France. One *hears* less about France in Germany than one does about Germany in France. Moreover, what really counts is not whether the bond between the two is tighter or looser but what they are able to achieve together. At the moment the answer is: not a great deal.

France has continued to flounder, although not to fall apart. In mid-November Chirac had an approval rating of 32 percent and Juppé of 18 percent. Rumors of Juppé's departure and of Séguin's becoming prime minister to inaugurate the by now mythical "other policy" were common in the German press[42] The wave of protest in the public sector has begun all over again, although it has not—or not yet—reached the 1985 level. Chirac has spent much time abroad. His Middle East trip was part of an attempt to reestablish a French and European presence, to strengthen France's role in Europe and Europe's role in the face of the U.S. Although Chirac's stand—if not his style—overlaps with recent Italian initiatives towards Iraq and Libya, there is little sign of a concerted EU policy towards the Middle East.

On November 24, the lira reentered the EMS amidst confused reports[43] that Germany and France had worked together or else that Germany had acted on France's behalf to ensure that the lira entered at a rate of 990 to the mark. Compared with the figures quoted above, this was a good rate for Italian exporters. However, it was perceived as a rate that the markets would test and that would allow no respite from the policy of rigor. The next day the press reported that Italy had, after all, received French support. The traditional alliance had been resurrected to allow Italy to return to the EMS and to allow France to play an intermediary role between the mark and the weaker Mediterranean currencies.[44]

If this represents business as usual, two events announced while this paper was being terminated were more striking, especially the second of them. First, Helmut Kohl announced his decision to lead his party into the 1998 parliamentary elections. It is obvious from our analysis that we do not regard this as any magic solution to Franco-German troubles or to Germany's own economic problems and the difficulties in meeting the Maastricht requirements. It may, however, have the unsought, but in our view desirable, result of driving the groups that oppose monetary union to organize better and to promote a more lively debate about Germany and Europe.

The second event was Jacques Chirac's April 21 announcement that parliament would be dissolved and elections held on May 25 and June 1. This was a gamble in the best Gaullist or Bonapatist traditions. Although there are considerations of domestic politics which cannot be discussed here for lack of space, Chirac is essentially asking his electorate, whose scepticism has increased since 1995, to allow him a free hand to cut government spending still further in the name of monetary union and to negotiate the organization of that union as well as the EU's institutional reforms.

The logic of Chirac's move is that the contemporary bargaining state must be strong at home, if it is to negotiate successfully within a regional bloc or an international body. To bargain in the context of parliamentary elections, which would normally be held in 1998, would weaken the French government's position. The gamble is that Chirac may sit down at the EU's negotiating table with a greatly reduced majority or a Socialist Prime Minister, which would weaken his position even more. An election allows the voters to express their opinions on a government's past performance and the Chirac-Juppé team has hardly excelled. It is unlikely that the center-right will have as large a majority as it had in 1993, but Chirac hopes to be able to claim that it is a majority specifically for austerity and monetary union. Since Chirac has, however, changed his mind so often, the electorate could legitimately wonder whether it was not merely giving him a free hand to do whatever he pleased.

One must admit that Chirac's willingness to gamble shows the importance he and his supporters ascribe to the overlapping issues of monetary union and cooperation with Germany. If Lionel Jospin holds to his initial position that a Left goverment would not make extra social cuts to meet the three percent target, that would stimulate a healthy debate in France and in Europa about the validity of such statistics.

Whatever happens, it appears likely that the Franco-German relationship will emerge from the doldrums as the deadlines for monetary union draw closer. The two countries will have to provide leadership because the sound and fury that accompany monetary union will grow more, rather than less, violent after the first group of countries is formed in spring 1998. The stakes are high because the financial markets will be watching closely and, if the EU does not demonstrate that it is in control, the consequences will be grave.

Notes

[1] "La France" is so often personified that it becomes a Madonna or a Fairy, which reveals the lyrical-mystical element in de Gaulle's discourse. But, while this element can never be ignored, he usually discusses the Franco-German relationship in the language of traditional diplomacy—people, nation and state. A group of nations may form an "organization," but not a community or a union. Charles de Gaulle, *Mémoires de Guerre: Le Salut, 1944-46* (Paris: Plon 1959), pp. 210, 184 and 113.

[2] *Le Salut,* p. 211.

[3] *Le Salut,* pp. 394-396.

[4] It is the weight given to foreign policy rather than the pursuit of a different policy that separates the Fifth from the Fourth Republic-Michael M. Harrison, *The Reluctant Ally: France and Atlantic Security* (Baltimore: Johns Hopkins University Press, 1981), chapter 1.

[5] *Le Salut,* p. 99.

[6] *Le Salut,* p. 101.

[7] *Le Salut,* p. 211.

[8] Twenty-nine percent of German exports went to EC members and 29 percent to other OECD nations. The figures for France were 25 and 16 percent, respectively. Germany had 8.1 percent of world exports and France 5.1 percent. For Adenauer's policy toward France, see Konrad Adenauer, *Erinnerungen 1945-'53* (Stuttgart: Deutsche Verlags-Anstalt, 1963), pp. 245 and 330-345. Adenauer constantly sought *Gleichberechtigung,* or equal treatment, for the fledgling German state.

[9] Harrison, *Reluctant Ally,* pp. 77-110.

134 PATRICK McCARTHY

[10] See Patrick McCarthy, "Condemned to Partnership," in *France-Germany 1983-1993: The Struggle to Cooperate* (New York: Saint Martin's Press, 1993), edited by Patrick McCarthy, p. 12.

[11] Pierre Messmer, "Notre politique militaire," *Revue de défence nationale,* May 1963, p. 761.

[12] The twenty-fifth anniversary of Nixon's dramatic announcement was on August 15, 1996. For a retrospective analysis, see *Le Figaro, économie,* August 15, 1996.

[13] Valéry Giscard d'Estaing, *Démocratie française* (Paris: Fayard, 1976), p. 123.

[14] See Patrick McCarthy, "France faces reality: rigor and the Germans," in *Recasting Europe's Economies,* edited by David Calleo and Claudia Morgenstern (Washington: University Press of America, 1990), pp. 25-78.

[15] For one report of this attempt, see *Der Spiegel* 18/1996 April 29, 1996, pp. 166-168.

[16] In France 61 percent of people favored German reunification, while 15 percent opposed it. In Britain the figures were 45 and 30 percent.

[17] For a succinct review of Chirac's career, see John Tuppen, *Chirac's France* (London: Macmillan, 1991), pp. 12-35.

[18] See Patrick McCarthy, *Between Europe and exclusion: the French presidential elections of 1995,* Johns Hopkins University Occasional Papers, 1996.

[19] *Le Monde,* December 14, 1994.

[20] There was no honeymoon. Chirac's approval rating fell by 11 percent in his first two months in office. Only 38 percent of people polled thought France was well governed, while 48 percent thought the opposite—*Le Monde,* July 27, 1995. But it was Juppé who had to face the hot autumn of 1995.

[21] "Discours du Président de la République à l'occasion de la réception des ambassadeurs," August 31, 1995. Text obtained from Service de Presse, Présidence de la République, pp. 1-6.

[22] For Chirac's speech, see *Le Monde,* October 28, 1996.

[23] "A Survey of France," *Economist,* November 25, 1995, p. 6.

[24] *Le Figaro,* July 6, 1996.

[25] *Le Monde,* July 16, 1996.

[26] Philippe Séguin, "Why France's Nuclear Plan Is Serious," *International Herald Tribune,* September 6, 1995.

[27] Philip H. Gordon, *France, Germany and the Western Alliance* (Boulder: Westview Press, 1995), pp. 83-101.

[28] *Le Figaro,* "Économie," August 29, 1996.

[29] See Alain Juppé's speech to the Institut des hautes études de défence nationale, *Le Figaro,* September 11, 1996.

[30] *Economist,* August 31, 1996, p. 23.

[31] *Le Figaro,* August 30, 1996.

[32] Luigi Spaventa, *Italy Enters the EMS,* JHU Bologna Center Occasional Papers, pp. 76-110.

[33] Beniamino Andreatta, *La Repubblica,* October 1, 1993.

[34] Spaventa, *Italy Enters the EMS.*

[35] Many figures were bandied around. The dispute is covered well in *La Stampa,* October 1-4.

[36] For an outline of this project, see *Le Monde,* September 25, 1996.

[37] *Die Frankfurter Allgemeine,* October 12 and 20, 1996.

[38] *Ibid.*

[39] *Le Monde,* October 5, 1996.

[40] See "German Survey," *Economist,* November 9, 1996, p. 9.

[41] *Economist,* January 4, 1997, p. 27.

[42] *Die Frankfurter Allgemeine,* November 12, 1996.

[43] *La Stampa,* November 25, 1996.

[44] *La Stampa,* November 26, 1996.

CONTRIBUTORS

Gilles Andréani is Director of the Center for Analysis and Planning (CAP) at the French Ministry of Foreign Affairs. He has served in Brussels as Deputy Permanent Representative of France to the North Atlantic Council. He also served as Deputy Head of the Planning Staff (DEG) at the French Ministry of Defense and as Head of the Disarmament Division within the Department of Strategic Affairs and Disarmament in the Ministry of Foreign Affairs. He is a graduate of the Institut d'Etudes Politiques in Paris and of the Ecole Nationale d'Administration.

David P. Calleo (Introduction and co-editor) is Dean Acheson Professor and Director of European Studies at the Paul H. Nitze School of Advanced International Studies (SAIS) of the Johns Hopkins University (Washington, D.C.). He received his B.A., M.A. and Ph.D. degrees from Yale University; has taught at Brown and Yale Universities, has been a Research Fellow at Nuffield College and a Visiting Professor at Columbia University, the College of Europe, the University of Munich, the University of Puget Sound, the University of Virginia, and the Institut d'Etudes Politiques de Paris. He has also served as consultant to the U.S. Undersecretary of State for Political Affairs. He has published extensively on political and economic issues concerning Europe and the United States. His books include *America and the World Political Economy*, with Benjamin Rowland; *The German Prob-*

lem Reconsidered; The Imperious Economy; Beyond American Hegemony: The Future of the Atlantic Alliance; and *The Bankrupting of America.*

François Heisbourg is Senior Vice President for Strategic Development at Matra Defense. Before that he was Director of the International Institute of Strategic Studies (IISS) in London. He has held various positions in the French government, including International Security Adviser to French Minister of Defense, Mr. Charles Hernu, and First Secretary at the French Mission to the U.N. in charge of international security issues and outer space affairs. His contributions appear in numerous publications on defense and strategic studies, including *Western Europe and the Gulf* and *The Shape of the New Europe.* He is a graduate of the Institut d'Etudes Politiques in Paris and of the Ecole Nationale d'Administration.

Klaus-Peter Klaiber is Head of Policy Planning in the Ministry of Foreign Affairs of Bonn. He has been Deputy Political Director in the Ministry of Foreign Affairs, and Deputy Head of Foreign Minister Genscher's Private Office. He has served at German embassies in London, Washington, D.C., Nairobi and Kinshasa. He holds a Law degree from Tübingen University, Federal Republic of Germany and a Ph.D. in Law from the University of Mainz, Federal Republic of Germany.

Jean-Pierre Landau is a graduate of the Ecole des Hautes Etudes Commerciales (HEC), the Institut d'Etudes Politiques in Paris, and the Ecole Nationale d'Administration, has held several positions in the French civil service, and is a former Adjunct Professor in the European Studies Department at the Paul H. Nitze School of Advanced International Studies of the Johns Hopkins University.

Patrick McCarthy is Professor of European Studies at SAIS and teaches at its Bologna Center. He holds a B.A. and D. Phil. from Oxford University and an A.M. from Harvard University. Before coming to SAIS he taught at Cambridge University and Haverford

College. He has also worked as a consultant on European labor relations. The author and editor of several studies, he has recently edited *France-Germany 1983-1993: The Struggle to Cooperate* and *The Crisis of the Italian State.*

Eric R. Staal (co-editor) is a Ph.D. candidate in the Department of European Studies at SAIS. He holds an M.A.L.D. from the Fletcher School of Law and Diplomacy at Tufts University and a B.A. in Political Science and German Studies from the University of California, Santa Barbara.

Michael Stürmer is Director of Stiftung Wissenschaft und Politik in Ebenhausen, Federal Republic of Germany. He has taught at the London School of Economics, the Sorbonne, the Center for International Studies at the University of Toronto/Canada, the University of Berlin, and the Friedrich-Alexander-Universität in Erlangen-Nürnberg. He has also been an advisor to the EU Commission and to the General Secretary of the Council of Europe. His more recent publications include *Das Ruhelose Reich: Deutschland 1866-1918 and Die Grenzen der Macht: Die Begegnung der Deutschen mit der Geschichte.*

Ernst Welteke is President of the *Landeszentralbank* of the State of Hesse, Federal Republic of Germany. He has also served as Minister of Finance and Minister of Economics, Transport and Technology in the State Government of Hesse. He holds a diploma in Economics from the Johann Wolfgang Goethe University in Frankfurt am Main.

INDEX

141